The Belgians in Manitoba

The Belgians in Manitoba

Keith Wilson
James B. Wyndels

Peguis Publishers Limited

Winnipeg, Manitoba

Canadian Cataloguing in Publication Data

Wilson, Keith, 1929-
   The Belgians in Manitoba

   Includes bibliography.
   ISBN 0-919566-52-9
   ISBN 0-919566-53-7 pa.

   1. Belgians in Manitoba.   I. Wyndels,
James B., 1945-   II. Title.
FC3400.B2W54   301.45'13'93207127
F1065.B4W   C76-016072-4

Printed and bound in Canada

Contents

Illustrations

Maps

Acknowledgements

This book was undertaken as a project by the Belgian History Committee to mark the 75th anniversary of the foundation of Le Club Belge. Thanks are due to all the members of this committee: Leonard De Baets, Marguerite De Baets, Jean D'Haese, André Janssens, Nora Renaud and Muguette Schorpion. The research assistance of Sheila Grover, Allan Peterkin and Daniel Woolf is gratefully acknowledged, as is the advice of Robert Painchaud, the assistance of Cecilia Ungrin and André Janssens in translations from the Flemish, and the photographic work of Leonard De Baets.

The publication of this book was made possible by generous grants from Le Club Belge and the St. Boniface Community Committee.

Louis De Nobele

Preface

OF ALL THE GROUPS which together constitute the ethnic mosaic of Manitoba, the Belgians are among the least known. This has occurred as a result of various historical factors.

In total numbers, Belgian immigrants to Manitoba remained comparatively small, so that today their descendants probably do not exceed 7000. Furthermore, their identification has always been made more difficult by the fact that they spoke either French or the Dutch-related Flemish, and that early Belgian immigrants were therefore frequently classified as French or Dutch.

There was also a natural tendency for French-speaking Belgians to merge with the French Canadians and to lose their separate identity; Flemish Belgians tended to assimilate readily with both French and English-speaking Canadians. If the Belgians themselves had problems of identification, it is not surprising that they lacked recognition by other groups.

Yet despite these problems and their small numbers, the Belgians have retained some characteristics and customs which are worthy of more general recognition.

The purpose of this book is simply to relate in outline the story of the arrival of Belgian immigrants to Manitoba and of their way of life, and thus to draw attention to the contributions of one of the smaller groups to the development of the province.

CHAPTER I

Belgium: The Historical Background

BELGIUM has existed as a distinct and independent state only since 1830, but the roots and traditions of the nation and its people reach back into the earliest recorded history of western Europe.

The Belgae, an ancient Celtic tribe from which modern Belgians take their name, were conquered in the first century B.C. by the Romans under whose rule they enjoyed material prosperity and later became Christians. Four centuries of Roman rule produced a mingling of races and cultures which continued even after the collapse of the Roman Empire in the fifth century. By this time, the Romanized Walloons and the Germanic Flemings had emerged as distinct groups with differing languages and characteristics. Their land, however, later became an integral part of the kingdom of the Franks and the centre of Charlemagne's empire. The peace and prosperity of Charlemagne's reign did not long survive his death in 814, and by 843 his empire had been divided, with Belgium as a buffer state between the future France and Germany. Belgium again became a scene of strife, the severity of which was compounded by the pillaging raids of the Norsemen who were finally defeated at Louvain in 891.

1

During the middle ages the power of the Emperor gradually declined, and princes and cities within the Empire increasingly asserted their independence. Belgian trade and industry, based initially on cloth and later on lace, glass and printing, began to flourish. A prosperous middle class emerged. The increasing power and influence of this commercial class brought about a tradition of communal autonomy which has long remained a characteristic feature of Belgian administration.

The power of the craft guilds was strikingly demonstrated in 1302 when an untrained Flemish militia, consisting largely of guild members, defeated a professional force of French and Flemish cavalry at the Battle of the Golden Spurs, named for the spurs supposedly taken from the defeated nobles. The date of this battle, July 11, has since been celebrated as the Flemish national holiday.

Belgian cities not only prospered as commercial and manufacturing centres, but also became centres of a cultural and intellectual renaissance typified by the foundation of the renowned University of Louvain in 1425. This prosperity reached its height during the period of Burgundian rule from 1384 to 1555. In this latter year the Emperor Charles V, who had inherited the Burgundian lands and who had been born in Ghent, abdicated and passed the Burgundian inheritance to his son, Philip II of Spain. Charles V, indeed, was the last native born ruler of Belgium until 1865.

The Burgundian lands had included both modern Belgium and the Netherlands, and the history of these two future nations continued to be closely interwoven. The new ruler had little sympathy for the attitudes and aspirations of his subjects in the Low Countries which he seldom visited and which he ruled through a series of Spanish governors. Philip's determination to impose absolute Spanish rule and to stamp out Protestantism, which was gradually spreading in the northern provinces, led inevitably to the eruption of civil war in 1567.

The civil war was complicated by the mutual distrust of the Catholics and Protestants, despite their common resentment of Spanish rule. In 1579 the northern provinces united and two years later proclaimed their independence. Though this independence was still far from secure, the action marked an irreparable cleavage in the Low Countries. Spanish power was still entrenched in the southern provinces which, through skillful diplomacy and loyalty to the Catholic church, became reconciled to a continuance of rule by Spain. Though war with the northern provinces continued intermittently, the independence of the Netherlands was finally recognized by the Treaty of Westphalia in 1648.

While Belgium remained under Spanish rule as the Spanish Netherlands, it increasingly became a battlefield and a pawn in the wars of Louis XIV with Spain and the independent Netherlands. By the Treaty of Utrecht, which ended the War of the Spanish Succession in 1713, Belgium was ceded to Austria and henceforth became known as the Austrian Netherlands. Though benevolent, Austrian rule was increasingly resented. The radical reforms of Emperor Joseph II, who attempted to curb the influence of the Catholic church and to curtail traditional government autonomy, caused open rebellion in 1789. Essentially conservative and aristocratic, the rebellion failed but nevertheless revealed within the Belgian people deep social rifts which were widened by the encroaching egalitarianism of the French Revolution.

In the wars between Austria and revolutionary France, Belgium again became a battleground before being formally annexed to France in 1795. Under the authoritarian and centralizing tendencies of French rule, the Belgians had no freedom but did enjoy a few years of internal peace and relative prosperity occasioned by French military needs. After this, Belgium was again ravaged by war until 1815 when Napoleon met final defeat on Belgian soil at Waterloo.

At the Congress of Vienna the map of Europe was redrawn in the interests of continental peace and security. Belgium was arbitrarily united with the Netherlands so that the United Netherlands could act as a strong buffer state to prevent future French expansion; and although this unification was neither popular nor long lasting, it nevertheless brought Belgium into the mainstream of European politics more prosperous, more centralized and more united in national consciousness.

Although the unification brought some economic and commercial benefits to the Belgians, the enlightened and well-intentioned reforms of the Dutch king provoked resentment among the mass of the people. Beneath all this lay a deep-rooted Belgian dislike of Dutch interference and Dutch rule.

For fifteen years there was constant friction. The Belgians were excluded from most official posts, and the constitution was heavily weighted in favour of the Dutch. The government's determination to make Dutch the official language of the entire nation provoked further resentment and also gave impetus to a quiescent Flemish movement. Furthermore, the Catholic bishops vigorously opposed government plans to grant religious toleration and to secularize the educational system.

The intransigence of the Dutch king drove rival Belgian factions into temporary union. In 1830 news of the successful revolution in France sparked riots which developed into a full scale revolt, leading to a Belgian declaration of independence. After considerable dissension, the crown of the new nation was finally offered to Prince Leopold of Saxe-Coburg who was proclaimed king as Leopold I on July 21, 1831, a day since celebrated as Belgian Independence Day. There followed several years of internal reorganization and international uncertainty, but by 1839 Belgian independence and neutrality had been guaranteed by all the great powers of Europe. This guarantee was respected for seventy-five years.

The newly independent nation inherited both unifying and disruptive traditions from its past history. While the vast majority of Belgians were Catholic, the Flemings were more devout than the Walloons in their religion; and there was increasing opposition to clerical dominance especially among the Walloons. Moreover, the ethnic and linguistic differences of the Flemings and the dominant Walloons were a continuing source of discord. Despite this, however, Belgium's independence brought a flowering of the arts such as had not been seen since the Burgundian period.

Under the astute rule of Leopold I, Belgium continued its international neutrality, improved its international trading position, maintained internal stability and reformed local government and judicial procedures. Furthermore, the building of railways, the encouragement of industry in the south, and the modernization of agriculture in the north brought the nation firmly into the modern era. Though agriculture remained important, the economic base of the nation became essentially industrial. Economic liberalism and the production of wealth brought the new kingdom unprecedented domestic prosperity, but pre-occupation with material prosperity in turn caused other problems: the neglect of external affairs and of domestic social conditions which encouraged the spread of socialism.

The languages of Belguim

from Mallison, *Belgium*, courtesy Ernest Benn Limited and Praeger Publishers Inc.

Leopold II, who became king in 1865, inherited his father's astuteness but had difficulty in winning the co-operation of his successive Liberal and Catholic govern-ments which remained overly concerned with such domestic issues as clerical influence in the school system, electoral reform, and language rights. While the educational issue could not readily be solved, universal male suffrage with a system of plural voting was introduced in 1893, and five years later Flemish was recognized as the second official language along with French.

Leopold's main interests lay in the acquisition of a colon-ial empire and in military preparedness. Stanley's explora-tions in central Africa won his enthusiastic support, and a company which he established brought him personal control over the Congo in 1885. Only after his business acumen had amply demonstrated its potential riches did the Belgian government in 1908 finally agree to annex the territory. The government also belatedly took steps to im-prove military preparedness by enacting a conscription law in 1909, the year of the king's death.

The prosperity in the period from the 1890's to 1914 had not been shared by the working classes whose demands grew more vociferous. Two new political parties, the Chris-tian Democrats and the Social Democrats, reflected these demands for social reforms, including the introduction of universal suffrage and universal compulsory education. Attempts at reform, however, were temporarily thwarted by the outbreak of the First World War and the German occupation of most of the country.

The German occupation, though hardly as severe as that of the Second World War, nevertheless had serious effects on the Belgian economy. But it also had a unifying effect on the people, despite their differences of language and social class. Constitutional and electoral reforms quickly followed the ending of the war, as the nation struggled to unite its people and restore its national and international position. The great depression of the 1930's, however, was felt as deeply in Belgium as elsewhere in the world.

In 1934, in the midst of economic troubles and consequent social and political unrest, the popular King Albert was accidentally killed and was succeeded by his son, Leopold III. The new king inherited an increasingly confused political situation in which linguistic differences were again surfacing and in which political extremism was becoming more apparent. Political disarray continued despite the threatening signs from Germany, and the nation was ill prepared to meet the German invasion in 1940. Effective Belgian resistance lasted little more than two weeks, the king surrendered and became a prisoner, and the government fled into exile.

The exiled government continued to lend active support to the allied cause, while in occupied Belgium the work of the underground resistance brought ruthless German retaliation. With the invasion of Europe, the allied armies rapidly pushed into Belgium, and the exiled government returned to Brussels before the final German surrender.

After the war, Belgium rapidly stabilized its currency, checked inflation, and made an economic recovery. Successive governments actively embarked on a series of reforms, such as a system of social security and an extension of the franchise to women in 1948. Settlement of the school question remained more elusive, however, until a compromise reached in 1958 brought state support for both Catholic and secular schools. Wartime disagreements over the king's surrender again brought to the surface basic constitutional problems. In 1951 these forced Leopold's abdication in favour of his son, Baudouin, and also brought a clarification of the role of the monarch who still retains considerable influence as a political arbiter.

In the post-war years, Belgium actively co-operated with its European neighbours in economics and defence, and has become a full partner in such organizations as NATO and the European Common Market, both of which have their headquarters in Brussels. This has brought not only increased economic prosperity but also a growing importance in international affairs.

Culturally rich and materially prosperous, despite the loss of the Congo which achieved independence in 1960, Belgium today is a nation which is manifestly a creature, and to some extent a captive, of its past. Although Belgium is now a constitutional monarchy, with a bicameral legislature and universal adult suffrage, the nation's heritage is reflected both in its traditions of strong local government and in its ethnic and linguistic divisions. These divisions which tend to parallel geographical and occupational differences and to influence electoral voting patterns, have been a determining factor in Belgian history since independence. The opposing concepts of a unitary and a federated state cannot be reconciled, and this has been recognized by the creation of linguistic areas and the acceptance of two official languages.

The issue has been further resolved by the creation in 1968 of separate government ministries in matters closely

related to the aspirations of the Walloons and the numeri-
cally stronger Flemings and of relationships between them.
It has aptly been claimed that the various differences in
Belgium are both complex and multi-dimensional, and that
these differences produce a multi-dimensional field of ten-
sion in which religious, ethnic, institutional, economic and
political philosophies constantly vary and interact.

Belgium is a young nation with old traditions. Like the
people of other nations in western Europe, the Belgians
have suffered political, social and religious strife and have
experienced vast agricultural and industrial change. Their
thrift and hard work have enabled them not only to cope
with their historical problems and achieve general prosperity in an over-populated land, but also to develop a rich
intellectual and cultural heritage along with a marked
ability to enjoy themselves. These achievements and these
characteristics have made the Belgians welcome immigrants
in many lands, and not least in Manitoba.

CHAPTER II

Belgian Immigration to Manitoba

W HEN the province of Manitoba was established in 1870 it was essentially a French-English duality. Its population numbered about 12,000 of whom slightly more than half were French-speaking and Roman Catholic; and the Manitoba Act included guarantees for the French language and Roman Catholic schools. There was, in fact, a general assumption that Manitoba would remain largely French in character and would continue to attract French-speaking settlers.

This assumption soon proved incorrect, as three demographic trends completely transformed the situation. The first was the large-scale movement of settlers from Ontario which poured 50,000 English Protestant farmers into Manitoba between 1871 and 1881. The second was the coming of such non-French and non-Catholic groups as the Mennonites and the Icelanders. The third was the withdrawal of many Métis from the province to better hunting grounds on the banks of the Saskatchewan River. These three trends combined to reduce the proportion of French-speaking people in Manitoba and to threaten the future rights of those who remained.

11

This threat was fully realized by Archbishop Taché who in 1876 observed to one of his priests, "Nous sommes débordés de toutes parts par des hommes qui ont la force, l'énergie, le nombre et la haine au coeur." Accordingly, he set about to bring the balance back to his favour by organizing societies and individual members of the clergy to obtain settlers from Quebec and the New England states where many former Québecois had gone to seek economic advantages. Neither of these attempts met with any degree of success, so Taché increasingly looked to Europe, especially France, Belgium, Germany and Ireland. Religion, apparently, had become almost as important as language in his plans for the future settlement of the province.

These new attempts by Taché coincided with the federal government's new immigration policy aimed at settling western Canada. To encourage the rapid building of the west, the government campaigned aggressively and established a network of government, private and corporate agencies to lure immigrants. Taché was able to ride on the coat-tails of this increased government activity.

For the prospective immigrant from Europe, Canada offered many attractions including responsible and liberal government, civil and religious liberty, security of life and property, and low taxation. Probably more immediately attractive than any of these was the offer of free land as homesteads. For many thousands of people in the overcrowded countries of Europe, this was too much to refuse.

The rising tide of anti-Catholic feeling in Western Canada, caused in part by the Métis uprising of 1885, made Taché all the more determined not to leave Catholic immigration to chance, and he accordingly heightened the immigration activities of the Church in Europe.

Although individual Belgian families first arrived in Manitoba in 1888, the first large group of 200 came in the following year partly through the efforts of Father Clouthier, an agent for Taché. Many of these settled in previously established rural French-speaking communities. The Dominion Intelligence Officer in Winnipeg reported that there was no lack of employment for those willing to work, and he noted in particular that southern Manitoba was especially suited for mixed farming to which Belgian farmers were well accustomed.

The Church and the government agreed on one thing: they wanted agricultural settlers, not immigrants from the industrial cities. The Church had additional reasons for this preference, for the Catholic Church in Belgium was facing an increasing opposition from urban liberals and anti-clericals. Understandably, the Church in Manitoba would prefer immigrants from the more traditional and conservative rural areas of Belgium. One priest commented succinctly:

> It is important to select colonists who have pecuniary resources, and within the Christian centres, for immigrants without religion and without principle rather impoverish a nation than improve it. It is not so much the quantity than the quality that has to be looked for.

The year 1890 saw a decline of British immigration to Canada and an influx of other nationalities including Belgians. J. E. Tetû was appointed as a government immigration agent to France and Belgium, and he reported that the class of immigrants was generally reasonably well-off, some having "considerable wealth."

Initial attempts to lure immigrants had considerable success, and by 1892 there were rural Belgian settlements in Deloraine and in the area of St. Alphonse, Swan Lake, Mariapolis and Bruxelles. Predictably, the immigrants were not universally welcomed, the *Deloraine Times* commenting in 1890:

> As for New Canada, our Grand North-West, let all newcomers learn English ... In the east let them 'parley-voo' as long as they like.

Not only was their welcome sometimes dubious, but many immigrants met hardships on their way from Belgium. It was said of one young Belgian woman coming to join her husband at Swan Lake:

> She travelled alone from Belgium, and as she could not speak one word of English she wore tags on her back and chest giving details of her identity, her destination in this country, and the means by which she was to travel. She was twenty-three days travelling, and in all that time could talk to no one.

Despite all their problems the settlements soon flourished. In 1890, Louis Hacault, an eminent journalist from Belgium, visited St. Alphonse and reported in very favourable terms of the conditions there:

> J'ai visité une vingtaine de familles. Tous les colons sont très contents. La femme Decalvaer m'a dit: 'Nous sommes ici dans le ciel!' Un autre

> m'a déclaré : 'C'est un paradis en été pour les
> hommes et pour les bêtes !'
> L'immense majorité fait ses devoirs religieux,
> malgré l'éloignement de l'église. Quelques-uns
> doivent faire trois ou quatre lieues pour aller à
> la messe. La moralité est très bonne. On se marie
> très jeune. Les familles de dix et onze enfants
> sont communes ici . . .

The journalist was so impressed, in fact, that he himself
later returned from Belgium as a settler.

One important means of recruiting immigrants was the
use by the federal government of 'return men,' men sent
to their homeland for the purpose of persuading their
friends and relatives to return with them. In an attempt
to improve the system, these men were to be put on
commission. It was proposed that each man would be paid
$8 for each eligible homesteader who could be convinced
to deposit $10 as a sign of good faith with the Department
of the Interior. Upon arrival in Canada the settler would
be returned his $10 deposit and would receive a small
additional sum. After getting ten people under the scheme,
the 'return man' would then be paid for his passage back
to Canada.

This system did not enjoy much success because prospective immigrants were seldom willing to put up an additional
$10 over and above the considerable cost of moving their
families, yet despite this, the 'return man' system continued
under various forms until 1898. Not untypical were these
two reports on the activities of these men:

> Leon Tinant — Went to Belgium, Department
> is not aware of address, and has no report from

> him whatever. His efforts have not produced any
> intending settlers, declaration or deposits.

> Charles Redberg . . . 12 Rue de l'Association,
> Brussels — Has not reported to the Department,
> and has as yet produced no evidence of work.

Generally more effective was the work of government agents, one of whom, August Bodard, described in detail his methods of recruitment:

> I canvassed only the country, going by carriage
> village to village and giving nearly every night
> free illustrated lectures on Canada like ... the
> C.P.R. lectures. During the projection of the
> views I explained all the advantages of Canada
> for farmers and afterwards distributed pamphlets
> to all those who asked, and answered every ques-
> tion made to me ... This work must be continued
> by the same agent 2 or 3 years, to bring the best
> results.

Bodard also wrote and distributed a very effective pamphlet which employed the technique of attracting interest by reproducing letters sent home by Belgian settlers. His principal concern, apart from praising the country and the integrity of the Belgian settlers already established, was to dispel rumours of the negative aspects of Canada. For example, the pamphlet assured the prospective emigrant that one of the charms of life in Canada was its wonderful climate; while it is true that the winters are harsh, he wrote, they are very short!

In 1895 Bodard rewrote and revised his Belgian propaganda and received government sanction for a 32-page *Guide*

du Colon Français, Belge et Suisse. This pamphlet devoted
several pages to the general conditions of life in Canada
including such topics as the form of government, relation-
ship of church and state, communications, public services,
naturalization procedures, and general facts and figures on
agriculture. In bold lettering Bodard then announced the
real reasons why Belgians should come to Canada.

POUR RIEN   64 HECTARES   (160 ACRES)
Pour les cultivateurs, le Canada est un des plus
beaux pays du monde.

The pamphlet goes on to describe accurately the responsibilities of a homesteader, and dwells on the glorious advantages of a land where a man with almost no money
can build up a grand existence through the fruits of his
own labour. Faith in God and pioneer perseverance were
the only necessities. Again, the pamphlet attempts to dispel
the concept of Canada as a frozen wasteland; two entire
pages are expended to describe how dry and clean the
winters are, how lovely is the crisp snow, and how the
climate rejuvenates the land for the productive summers.
There are no plagues and no dangerous reptiles in Canada,
the pamphlet assures, and the Indians are safely away on
reservations.

Bodard's idea of wooing immigrants by publishing letters
from successful and happy settlers was a particularly effective technique, for first-hand reports are usually persuasive
and have an air of authenticity even if they do not always
give a wholly accurate picture. In 1894 the Canadian
government published an entire booklet of these letters,
all dated and signed. Most of the farmers who contributed

An early immigration poster

were Walloons residing in Manitoba or the Northwest
Territories, and the letters were collected for the Department of the Interior by Father Willems, the parish priest
at Bruxelles. All the letters were in French, and were concerned mainly with farming conditions and prospects.
Typical of many was that of Joseph Massoz of Bruxelles,
addressed to Father Willems.

> Bruxelles, Manitoba,
> le 24 novembre, 1893
> Monsieur, — Ma famille se compose de sept
> personnes. J'ai quitté Grand Mesnil, en Belgique,
> le 14 mars 1888, et je suis arrivé ici le 2 avril
> suivant; je n'avais plus que huit piastres à mon
> arrivée, et j'ai commencé par travailler rudement,
> à des pris variant d'une piastre à une piastre et
> 50 centins par jour.
> Je suis établi sur le sud-est de la section 16,
> township 6, rang 11; j'ai 35 acres en culture, le
> restant de ma terre est en bois et en foin; j'ai
> bâti une maison, une *grainerie* et plusieurs étables;
> ma terre a une valeur actuelle de 900 piastres,
> et j'ai en outre tous les instruments agricoles, je
> tiens 9 bêtes à cornes et 4 chevaux.
> Six années d'experience en ce pays m'ont
> prouvé que l'élevage des animaux combiné avec
> la culture est ce qui paie le mieux. En hiver,
> le commerce du bois est une grande ressource
> pour le Belges établis ici: l'hiver dernier, j'en ai
> conduit à Holland pour 308 piastres et je crois
> en conduire davantage cet hiver.
> Je trouve l'air de ce pays très vif et sain. Les
> Belges établis ici jouissent d'une aisance qu'ils
> n'auraient pu espérer en Belgique. Les Canadiens
> se distinguent par l'hospitalité qu'ils exercent
> envers les étrangers.
> Joseph Massoz

In addition to the work of immigration agents, prospective emigrants in Belgium received guidance from La So-

ciété St. Raphael which was organized in 1888 by a group
of laymen to assist Belgian emigrants who were bound for
Canada or South America. The society contacted Archbishop Taché in order to locate local representatives to
receive the immigrants and help them to get established,
and later, in 1895, petitioned the Canadian government
for assistance in bringing out six scouts to get a clear idea
of what exactly they were promoting. Although it is not
known whether or not the delegation actually came, there
was continued pressure both from the Society and from the
Hamburg-American Line for more federal financial support
of intending immigrants.

In 1898 Treau de Coeli, a Belgian from Quebec, was
appointed official Canadian government agent to Belgium
and Holland. He was a careful and thorough man who,
before taking his appointment overseas, came to the west
to familiarize himself with the conditions and problems
of Belgian settlers. On the whole, he found them happy
and prosperous.

When he took up his posting in Belgium, de Coeli was
disappointed to find how little was known about Canada,
particularly in the northern Flemish-speaking provinces.
He therefore concentrated on the recruitment of Flemish
immigrants from the densely populated northern regions,
and this tendency continued thereafter. The ratio of urban
to rural immigrants correspondingly increased as did the
ratio of Flemish to French-speaking. By 1930 only about
25% of the Belgians entering Canada were French-speaking.
This ratio has since remained fairly static in Manitoba.

While de Coeli's appointment was in no way connected
with the Church, the Church continued its own efforts to

encourage suitable immigrants. While attending an overseas conference in 1898 Archbishop Langevin met a Belgian priest, Father Delouche, who had formulated a plan for emigration of his people in close-knit groups to Canada. He planned a society to purchase land for settlement and to assist immigrants with passage and initial expenditures. This organization, known as La Société d'exploration agricole du Canada, won the enthusiastic endorsement of Langevin who obtained the support of de Coeli, petitioned the C.P.R. to determine available lands, and urged both Laurier and Sifton to back the project. After some delay, four prominent Belgians came to Canada in 1900 as a delegation to study the possibilities of bloc agricultural settlement and reported favourably on the prospects.

Then in May 1901, Delouche informed Langevin that the project was facing financial difficulties as Belgium was experiencing a commercial and industrial depression which would delay the project indefinitely.

The financial difficulties were never overcome. Both Langevin and Delouche were bitterly disappointed in the failure; Delouche would not see groups of Belgians settled in prospering and faithful communities in western Canada, and Langevin missed the opportunity of adding to the French-speaking population in his area.

In 1900 the acting Minister of the Interior, James Sutherland, gave a hearty recommendation for the energetic work of Treau de Coeli, but it is extremely difficult to discern at this time exactly how successful were these attempts to attract Belgian immigrants. The difficulty lies in the statistical methods used by the Canada Census. Prior to 1901 the Belgians in Canada were too small a group to be listed separately and were therefore grouped with immigrants from France. Furthermore, prior to 1911 the immigrant entrance statistics are indicated by ports of entry, including American ports. There is thus no accurate method of determining the actual numbers of Belgians arriving yearly in Manitoba until 1911, although it is possible to estimate the number of people of Belgian origin living in the province.

In 1901 there were 940 people of Belgian ancestry in Manitoba; by 1911 there were 2,453. Some of these would be Canadian born, but nevertheless, the figures represent a considerable rate of immigration. The government agent was either doing a good job or was very lucky.

Not surprisingly, de Coeli reported that this increase was the result of his energies and convincing manner. He employed the acceptable techniques of the period in keeping with the government's need for agricultural immigration, and toured the northern provinces with a series of lectures and lantern slides in the small towns. He would then distribute the government propaganda and answer questions. The Canadian government also had displays at the major agricultural exhibitions to show the finest Canadian grains and other products to advertise the advantages of soil and climate to the European farmer.

Many of the government agents in Europe ran into opposition from the governments of the country in which they sought to recruit. This was not the case in Belgium. De Coeli took pains to explain that he carried out his work with the full knowledge and permission of the authorities and while they did not necessarily welcome the emigration of the populace, they did not oppose it. He knew very well how to avoid conflict with local authorities:

> At every one of my lectures, I made it a point to invite the civil authorities, and although I must admit that some parties are systematically opposed to emigration, I have always been able to convince them that it is beneficial to those who have necessary disposition and means and that instead of being prevented it should be helped and wisely counselled, consequently that it is in the interest of every one, that the advantages at least should be known.

De Coeli also knew where best to look for prospective immigrants. Every May, between 45,000 and 50,000 workers left Belgium to be hired as farm labourers in France. The majority of these men held tiny plots of land in Belgium, averaging from a half to two acres, which they left in the care of their families who would till the land for a meager crop. The men would return after harvest each fall with their wages to keep their families during the winter. If these families could raise the money required for passage, Canada would certainly present a brilliant prospect. Many of these families did in fact come to Manitoba.

By 1904 de Coeli had established himself in an office in Antwerp, from which all emigrants to Canada departed. Three years later the Minister of the Interior, Frank Oliver, inspected the office and found it unsuitable for the prestigious function it performed on behalf of the Canadian government. Oliver insisted that the offices be moved so as to be "a credit to Canada." De Coeli followed his wishes and one month later he opened in Antwerp "one of the

best Canadian government offices, decorated by grasses,
grain, stuffed fowls, (and) appropriate photos and prints."

De Coeli's other methods to attract prospective settlers
also deserve some attention. In 1905, for example, he
arranged a grand display on behalf of Canada at a universal
exhibition held in Antwerp in celebration of the 75th anniversary of Belgian independence; while in the following
year he brought over a group of six Belgian farmers to
assess the agricultural opportunities in Canada and to
report back favourably in their homeland.

In addition to placing advertisements in local newspapers, de Coeli printed and circulated a paper, *West
Canada,* at government expense. Published monthly in

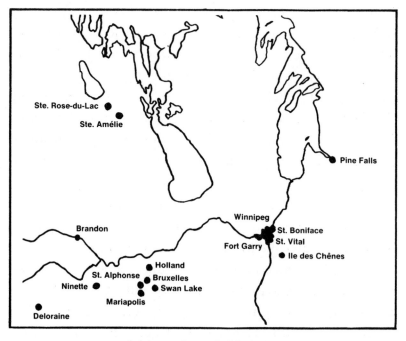

Belgian settlement in Manitoba

French and Flemish and distributed in both Belgium and Holland, the paper was apparently well received. De Coeli also had a pamphlet *The World's Best Wheat Fields*, published in both languages and distributed to 300,000 farmers, market gardeners, clergymen, school teachers and farm labourers.

The Canadian government also distributed atlases and encouraged the teaching of Canadian geography in schools both in Britain and continental Europe. By 1910 nearly 4,000 schools in Belgium taught some Canadian geography. De Coeli also circulated three sets of slides throughout the schools on request from interested teachers. So inspired were some of these teachers that they in turn gave lectures on Canada, which he described as "a journey through agricultural Canada, from the Atlantic to the Pacific Ocean, and lasts about two hours." This, combined with the popularity of literature glorifying frontier life of the New World, undoubtedly played a part in increasing interest in emigration especially among the young.

In 1911 a special agent for the Department of the Interior, Olivar Asselin, was sent out to determine the efficiency of the government office in Belgium. He later reported that while de Coeli was doing an excellent job, he was being hampered by the smallness of the operation which was run on a tight budget. In view of the excellent quality of Belgian immigrants and their contribution to mixed farming in Canada, Asselin recommended that no expense be spared in recruitment in that country. He also recommended that Belgium become a separate agency instead of being tied in with Holland, and that it should be withdrawn from the control of the High Commissioner in Britain. Until this time a greater effort had been made to attract immigrants from Britain, but it was from the continental nations that Canada was actually getting the kind of immigrants she wanted most. Even the High Commissioner in London admitted that British immigrants were not of particularly good quality.

The outbreak of the First World War presented further problems for immigration from Belgium. Considerable pressure was brought to bear on the Canadian government to accept thousands of refugees who had fled when Belgium was occupied by the Germans. Hundreds of people in western Canada offered assistance to families and orphans; and W. D. Scott, the Superintendent of Immigration, reported that he had many requests "for Belgian girls of tender years, who must be fair-haired, blue-eyed, bright, affectionate and good-looking."

The government, however, resisted this pressure. It was felt that large scale immigration would mean a significant loss to Belgium, and that it would in any case be difficult to cope with the extra burden which an influx of refugees would place upon an economy that was straining under the war effort. Moreover, the Belgian government vigorously opposed the emigration of anyone except women and children. By December 1914, the Belgian government officially stated that, in view of the serious depopulation of the country, it was not the wish of the Belgian government that "refugees of either sex should emigrate to Canada, or to any other distant part, from whence their return at the end of the war would be doubtful."

The Canadian government office in Antwerp closed, and

Belgian immigration dwindled to a total of 265 between 1915 and 1919.

After the war, the Belgian government refused passports to people in certain fields of employment, including agriculture. At the same time Canada permitted entry only to farmers with sufficient resources to allow them to farm without assistance from the government, or farmers who had friends or relatives who could guarantee them employment. Despite these regulations, a few industrial workers and other non-farmers did emigrate.

It was, however, farmers who were most wanted, and farmers from Belgium were still considered among the best. In 1920, Sifton wrote to J. W. Dafoe:

> The place to look for immigrants is Belgium, Denmark and in a greater degree Norway and Sweden. From these countries the best agricultural settlers can be procured, who are perfectly competent when they arrive in Canada to take care of themselves...

Pursuant to this, the Immigration Act was again revised, and stringent controls were placed on people seeking entry to Canada — $250 per family, plus $125 per person over 18 years, $50 per person under 18 years and an additional surcharge for immigrants arriving in the winter months. Although these regulations did not apply to verified farmers and their immediate families, or to domestic servants, immigration declined significantly and did not recover until the fees were removed in 1924.

As controls tightened, the need for careful screening and inspection meant that most of the continental government offices became largely inspectional centres. From 1922 to

1928, for example, the Antwerp office served only for preliminary inspection not so much intended to encourage the immigrant as had been the case before the First World War, but to advise intending immigrants and to check them through the government regulations. Official government policy was expressed by the High Commissioner, W. L. Griffith, in 1922:

> It has been our feeling since the beginning of the Great War that Belgium has suffered so much through devastation of the country and loss of population that it would be unfair to encourage the migration of her people to Canada unless that course would be favoured by the Belgian government. If Belgium at any time has a surplus for settlement in another country, Canada will be surely interested in securing a good share of these.

In effect, Canada's own priorities for development through agricultural colonization and Belgium's need of her own farming class combined to retard the recruitment of Belgians for Canada and Manitoba. Belgian immigration to Manitoba became a mere trickle: 258 people from 1916 to 1920, 211 people from 1921 to 1925, and 237 from 1925 to 1930. Not until after the end of the Second World War did immigration again reach the level prior to 1914. This can partly be explained by the fact that the federal government was more concerned with populating Saskatchewan and Alberta, and that the Church had ceased to take an active role in immigration. More recent Belgian immigration has tended to be on an individual basis and to include more from the better educated and urban population.

The Belgians in Manitoba are today not easily enumerated. Intermarriage has inevitably made it more difficult to define exactly what is meant by 'Belgian'; while the traditional linguistic problem has tended to obscure the difference of Walloon and French. Their settlement pattern has, however, not essentially changed. There are identifiable groups scattered in the small towns of the province particularly in areas suitable for mixed farming. These smaller settlements are largely to the west and south west of Winnipeg. From the days of the first immigrants, however, the centre of Belgian settlement has been the metropolitan area of Winnipeg and in particular St. Boniface, St. Vital and Fort Garry.

CHAPTER III
Le Club Belge/The Belgian Club

L E CLUB BELGE was formally incorporated in October, 1905, its name reflecting the fact that most Belgians, both Walloons and Flemings, could speak French. Its founding president was Louis De Nobele who, with his father-in-law, Theophiel Elewaut, first suggested the formation of the Club so that the Belgians, who were arriving in larger numbers every month, could gather, discuss their problems and find enjoyment among themselves.

The specific purposes and powers of the Club were detailed in its initial statute of incorporation under the Manitoba Joint Stock Companies Act in 1905. The petitioners sought incorporation as a company for the purpose and with the object of

(a) establishing, maintaining and conducting a club for the accommodation of members of the Company and their friends, and providing, furnishing and maintaining a club house and other conveniences, and generally to afford to members all the possible advantages, conveniences, and accommodations of a club.

(b) to permit the said club to be used by the members of the said Company and their friends either gratuitously or on such terms as shall be agreed upon and if thought fit to manage the affairs of the Club or any of them and generally to do what may seem best calculated to promote the interest of the Company and in particular, to lend money to or subsidize the clubs or Clubs.

(c) to provide and maintain a social intercourse between the members of the Company; to consider and discuss all questions affecting the interests of the Belgian residents in Manitoba, to procure delivery of lectures on any subject of interest to the Company; to form and maintain a library; to render voluntary aid or otherwise to any member of the Company or to any Belgian residing in Manitoba; to purchase, hire or otherwise acquire for the purpose of the Company any real or personal property, that is , land, buildings, furniture, books, household effects, musical instruments, apparatus, appliances, conveniences and accommodation.

(d) to mortgage, sell or otherwise dispose of any property real or personal belonging to the Company; to erect, maintain and improve or alter any buildings for the purpose of the Company.

(e) to borrow or raise money by the issue of bonds, debentures, debenture stock, bills of exchange, promissory notes or securities by mortgage or exchange upon any part of the property of the Company.

(f) to provide an entrance fee for any member of the Company and no person shall be able to be a member of the Company, or take shares in the said Company unless he is a Belgian by birth, exceptions being made for any Consul that may be appointed for the Province of Manitoba by the proper authorities.

The petitioners and charter members numbered 45 and included a wide representation of trades and occupations:

the fact that most Belgians were living in St. Boniface, the Club moved to that city. By borrowing money, the Club was able to build a hall on Provencher Boulevard which, with later modifications, has remained its home ever since. Rapidly increasing memberships enabled the mortgage to be repaid within two years. Finances continued in a healthy state for several years, amenities were improved and two additions were made to the original building.

The provincial government in 1916 passed legislation which extended the vote to women and enforced prohibition. Both decisions affected the Belgian Club. Although wives of members had always been welcomed to the Club, in July of that year the Club decided to admit other women if escorted by a member. Not until 1939, however, were women eligible for full membership. Prohibition had more serious consequences. Traditionally Belgians were beer drinkers, and beer drinking was an essential aspect of social intercourse. With prohibition, the Club inevitably lost some of its appeal and its operation became very difficult. These difficulties were compounded by the problems of the First World War and its immediate aftermath. A rapid succession of presidents deprived the Club of stable leadership, and the Club soon ran into financial difficulties. Expenses were curtailed, the Club was closed several days in the week, and a bank loan was obtained to pay the taxes.

In order to promote business and increase membership, a Congress for all Belgians in western Canada was held in February 1918. Although some 20 delegates from communities in Manitoba and Saskatchewan attended this meeting, there seems to have been little lasting effect. The Club consistently operated at a loss, and interest among

21 labourers, four contractors, four florists, three farmers, two bakers, two brick-layers, two carpenters, and one butcher, clerk, commercial traveller, delivery man, proprietor, restaurant keeper and stonecutter.

At its inception, then, the Belgian Club was widely representative of the Belgian population and had as its mandate the recreational, cultural, social and economic interests of the Belgian community in Manitoba. In practice, however, the interests of the Club always extended beyond the immediate needs of the Belgians and embraced, to some extent at least, the concerns of the community at large.

The Club's influence necessarily depended on its own strength, and to a remarkable degree the history of the Club reflected the problems and trends of the wider society. The first meetings were held in a boarding house on Lombard Street in Winnipeg, but in 1906, in recognition of

Original building of Le Club Belge, 1908

members continued to lag. By 1922 it was decided to close
the Club and rent the building, but even the tenants could
not meet their financial obligations and the Club's position
further deteriorated.

A special meeting in January 1925 initiated decisive
action to save the Club by invoking the clause in the Club's
charter of incorporation in 1907 which permitted the levy-
ing of an annual fee on members. This fee was fixed at
25¢ per month payable in advance. These new financial
arrangements, the end of prohibition in 1928, and the
undertaking of other means of raising money enabled the
Club not only to survive but further to expand its activities
despite the problems caused by the long depression in the
1930's.

Just prior to the outbreak of the Second World War,
a branch of the Club was established in the largely Belgian
community of Ste. Rose-du-Lac. This branch continued
in active operation until 1949. The main Club flourished
throughout the war years, and its improved financial status
enabled it to build a further extension to its premises in
1948.

The last two decades have seen a continued growth of
the Club which by the early 1970's had over 2600 share-
holders and over 500 associate members. This growth has
enabled the Club to extend its services in support of the
many aspects of Belgian life in the province.

The work of the Club, and its contribution to the Belgian
community in Manitoba, must be assessed in terms of the
aims and responsibilities set out in its charter. As has been
seen, these included the recreational and social, cultural,
and economic interests of the Belgian immigrants.

From the very beginning, an attempt was made to provide recreational facilities within the Club. Even before the Club moved into its own building, it had rented a billiard table. Later, in 1913, the Club purchased its own table, and with the formation of a Billiard Club, billiards and pool have since remained a popular pastime.

Similarly, facilities for card games were provided as early as 1905. Interest apparently lagged, however, and by 1917 the president of the Club appealed for better attendance at the monthly card and billiard contests. Card competitions for men and women were well established by the following year, and by 1926 Sunday whist drives were organized over the winter months to aid the Club's finances. Some of these were apparently conducted under the auspices of the Belgian church which received the proceeds.

While card games retained their popularity, they were later surpassed as money-raisers by dances and, more recently, by bingo. Dances were held in the new hall as early as 1907, and by 1917 they were regularly sponsored by the Club and its affiliated organizations. Concerts were also regular attractions by this time, and both were intended to draw the Belgians together and make the Club the focal point of Belgian community life. Special concerts, dances and parties were held to raise money for specific charitable purposes, but most proceeds went to the Club or to the sponsoring organization.

The popularity and financial success of dances in the financially troubled years of the 1920's and 1930's is indicated by the fact that by 1937 regular dances were being sponsored by as many as 19 affiliated clubs. Dances, parties and concerts continued throughout the Second World War and in the subsequent years when teenagers of Belgian descent were encouraged to make the Club the centre of their social activities. Bingo games, begun in 1953, had become regular weekly events by 1960, and, after producing a profit of over $3,000 in the first year, became a dependable source of income for the Club.

These various social gatherings, combined with the traditional Belgian proclivity for beer drinking, unfortunately often proved a source of embarrassment to the officials of the Club. There were regular suspensions of members for gambling, drunkenness, brawling, obscene language and unbecoming behaviour. These conditions may have been the reason for the formation in 1926 of a ladies' committee "to further the moral and material aspirations of the Club." If so, the committee seems to have had little noticeable effect.

In 1938 the parish priest suggested the enforcement of strict regulations to establish the good name and reputation of the Club, but his pleas apparently fell on deaf ears and the bad behaviour continued. A letter from the Club's executive in 1955 stated categorically that "under no circumstances is fighting to be tolerated at the Club," and a year later employees were given full authority "to refuse to serve beer to any patron, member or guest, entering the Club if such a patron, in their opinion, appears to be under the influence of liquor." Conditions still did not immediately improve, and by the following year arrangements were made for the payment of policemen attending parties and dances.

Although these deplorable events tended to give the Club a bad name, it must be remembered that they resulted from the actions of only a small minority, and that they were as embarrassing to the average Club member as they were to the general public.

The recreational interests of the Belgians naturally extended beyond the sports and pastimes provided within the Club building. Members of the Belgian community participated fully in non-Belgian sports such as baseball, athletics, hockey, curling, five and ten pin bowling, rifle shooting, football and hunting. In some of these activities, participants formed organizations in affiliation with the Belgian Club and received some financial support either by holding dances at the Club or by direct grants. These grants were not large, and some of the traditional Belgian caution in financial matters can be discerned, for example, in the condition attached to the support of the five-pin bowling team as recently as 1973 when the Club executive passed a motion that "The Club buy five shirts for the five-pin Belgian Club team and the shirts belong to the team and not the bowlers. The shirts to last for five years."

The Club also made small, but regular, donations to many community sports and recreational events; and these have increased with the improvement of the Club's finances in recent years.

Nor were the children and the older members forgotten. In 1926 the Club began a long tradition by providing a Christmas tree and presents for children of members; and the year 1931 saw the first of the regular annual parties for Belgians 60 years of age and over. The Ladies Get-Together Club, the Ladies Handicraft Society, and the Old Timers' Club long continued to serve the quieter social needs of the members.

Today, as the Belgian Club approaches its 75th anniversary, it has a total of 13 active affiliated clubs, some of which involve Belgians living in the smaller communities of the province.

Throughout its history, the Club has tried to protect the economic interests of the Belgians in Manitoba. This has been done in several ways: the establishment of organized societies, the giving of financial and other assistance to individual Belgians, and the continued support of charities for the benefit of the entire community. In the aftermath of the First World War, the Belgian Veterans' Associations was formed in 1920. This consisted of veterans who had been under fire on the battlefields of Europe. Later, in 1929, the Belgian Veterans' Society, open to all veterans and affiliated with the Royal Canadian Legion, was also formed. While the purposes of these groups were partly social, they were also partly concerned with the welfare of their members, and the Ladies' Auxiliary built up an impressive record of achievement in support of the education and general economic welfare of the families and children of veterans.

In 1926 the Ladies Auxiliary of the Belgian Club, later renamed the Belgian Ladies Sick Visiting Society, was founded by the Club president, Nicolas Pirotton. The members of this society, most of whom were tri-lingual, made a significant contribution during the depression years by bringing the needs of their people to the attention of the St. Boniface Relief Department and by providing clothing to the destitute. To defray operating expenses, the Society received special permission from the Belgian Club to sell hand-made roses at 10¢ each on the premises of the Club each Saturday, and it also held an annual dance. As each affiliated club was allotted one annual dance, a second organization, known as the Belgian Ladies Sick Visiting Association, was formed. For some years, the funds from two annual dances enabled operating expenses to be met.

Their work consisted mainly of visiting hospitals or homes for the elderly, wherever a member of the Belgian community was known to be. While still an active organization, the Belgian Ladies Sick Visiting Society is now wholly dependent on the Belgian Club for financial support.

The second organization primarily concerned with the economic interests of the Belgians was the Belgian Mutual Benefit Society. As many Belgian settlers arrived in Manitoba with few resources and skills, they intially accepted all types of employment in order to afford the necessities of life.

Low wages, seasonal lay-offs and the lack of any system of unemployment insurance caused considerable hardships. Especially hard times followed the death of a family wage-earner. When this occurred, the Belgian community usually asked a local leader to make a collection to defray at least the immediate funeral expenses. Many Belgians, however, balked at the acceptance of charity, and they decided to form a benefit society as a form of insurance. This Belgian Mutual Benefit Society was organized in 1928.

Initially, membership was restricted to those of Belgian ancestry, but as this proved a hardship to a member whose spouse was not Belgian, the restriction was later removed and membership was opened to associate members of the Belgian Club. The age limit was established at 45½ years.

Membership fees varied, but eventually the practice was adopted of each member paying $1.00 to the fund on the death of any member. Administered by a board of directors elected at the annual meeting of the Belgian Club, the Society has retained a membership of slightly under 500.

Throughout its history, the Belgian Club has also consistently helped members of the Belgian community on an individual basis. As early as 1915 the Club expressed concern for the plight of unemployed Belgians in St. Boniface and presumably did what it could to ease the situation. Again, in the late 1920's, Club members gave individual assistance to recent immigrants and also established an employment office in the Club. Members actively supported Belgian employees having difficulty at their place of work, and in 1928, the Club organized a committee specifically to promote and protect the interests of Belgian tradesmen.

This tendency among the Belgians to provide mutual support continued during the troubled times of the depression years. The Club actively protested the lay-offs at the CNR Transcona yards in 1938, and at the same time adopted the firm policy of purchasing all merchandise (except beer) from Belgian storekeepers so long as their prices were competitive. In 1936 the Club had further attempted to assist the younger Belgians by providing a $10.00 gift on the marriage of a member.

But general policies of assistance cannot take account of every individual case of hardship. In 1928, a box was placed in the Club for donations for needy Belgian families, and frequent special collections were made to defray costly medical expenses incurred by members and their families.

At no time did the Club ignore its responsibility to the

wider community; but although it frequently made small donations to a wide range of charities and community activities, it understandably gave first consideration to the needs of St. Boniface. Thus in 1934 it financed the construction of the attractive entrance gate at the Kiwanis Happyland Park on Marion Street, and it consistently supported the St. Boniface hospital in which it endowed a ward in 1953. More recently it has actively considered the building of a home for senior citizens.

The Belgian Club, by its very nature, served also as a focal point of Belgian ethnic consciousness in Manitoba; and as this consciousness developed, the Club became more politically active. As part of its mandate to build and retain a common sense of identity among the Belgians, the Club consistently sought to maintain some liaison not only with other Belgian communities within Manitoba, but also with communities elsewhere in Canada and in the United States. Parallel to this was the constant effort to maintain close ties with the mother country.

While much of the liaison with the smaller Belgian communities took place through sporting events, there were also more formal gatherings. Thus in 1918 there was a Congress of Belgians in Western Canada, and in 1921 a joint conference was organized with the Belgian Club of Montreal. Further liaison took place through the Belgian consuls in the major Canadian cities, but only with the affluent years after the Second World War and the increasing attention paid to ethnic minorities in the 1960's was there a re-awakening of interest in more direct contact with other Belgian communities. And so in 1963 three members of the Club attended the Congress of Belgium in the World at Ottawa. Subsequent meetings took place in Toronto, Montreal and again at Ottawa.

Understandably, the Club also constantly attempted to maintain close ties between the Belgian community in Manitoba and the mother country. For many years the most effective means of cultural communication with Belgium was through the *Gazette van Detroit* which was widely read in Manitoba. Initially published in Flemish, it was later written partly in Flemish and partly in English. Significant events in Belgian history were noted, and as early as 1910 it was decided to hold an annual celebration on July 11, the Flemish national holiday. In 1916 this was changed and henceforward the annual celebration was held on July 21, the Belgian Independence Day. While the proposed requiem mass for Leopold II in 1909 was post-poned apparently through lack of interest, the Club was otherwise punctilious in its relations with the Belgian government and royal family. Furthermore, the Club actively supported relief work in Belgium after the devastation of two world wars. More recently, the availability of cheap air travel has enabled many more Belgians to renew their ancestral ties, and this has tended to strengthen both their ethnic identity and their sense of Canadian pride.

Within the Club, with its majority of Flemish members, the inherited language problem long remained a source of contention. The original dominance of French was gradually weakened, and by 1915 the Club adopted the policy of reading all reports in both French and Flemish. The debates in the Legislative Assembly in 1916 aroused considerable interest among the Belgian community. The Club not only sent a letter of appreciation to the M.L.A.

for Ste. Rose-du-Lac who had defended multilingualism, but also passed a motion condemning, and accusing of hypocrisy, some Belgians who had opposed multilingualism.

Demands for more use of Flemish were again raised after the end of the First World War, and in the 1920's concentrated efforts were made to secure Flemish-speaking employees at St. Boniface city hall and post office. A certain disgruntlement with the French became apparent in 1927 when the Club sarcastically thanked *La Liberté* for ignoring the Belgian contribution to the Canadian diamond jubilee celebrations!

To the traditional linguistic conflict of French and Flemish was added the encroachment of the English language. This encroachment was rapid, and came about for both a positive and a negative reason.

English, being the dominant language of the province, inevitably gained ground especially among the younger Belgians, but it also gained further as a result of the traditional Belgian language conflict. By 1928 the new by-laws of the Belgian Club were printed in English, although notices of meetings were still in three languages. The final step in the language dispute within the Club occurred in 1943 with the decision to record all business in English.

But if the language dispute was settled within the Club and within Manitoba, it could still cause rancour at national meetings. As late as 1969 a representative from Manitoba to the Council of the Belgians in Ottawa reported:

> The predominance of the use of the French language plus the undercurrent tense feeling between the Flemish faction and the Walloon faction at these meetings prompted me to address

the meeting expressing my feelings on this matter
and requesting that the remaining portion of this
meeting, plus all future meetings, be conducted
in the English language basing my request on
the fact that the English language be used as
the common denominator of the other two
languages. This request was met with a great deal
of criticism directed at me from the President
as well as other members present. My reaction
to this criticism was to point out the fact that
I represented a 3,000 member club and a negative
reaction to my request could influence me into
making an unfavourable report to my Committee
which may have a bearing on our future participation in the Council. More serious discussion
took place on this matter and the participants
who had addressed the meeting and each other
in the French language suddenly started to speak
English. This complete change in attitude also
influenced the election which took place immediately after the discussion.

A Flemish President was elected who conducted the remaining portion of the meeting in
English and also stressed the fact that all future
meetings would be conducted in English with
Flemish and French translation available on request.

Because some Belgians were French-speaking Walloons
who tended to merge into the French element in society, the general public tended either to confuse all
Belgians with the French or to be completely unaware of
their existence. Similarly some Flemings complained that
they were too often counted as Dutch. One problem facing
the Belgians, therefore, was simply to win recognition as
a group and to attract public notice. This was tackled in
two ways: by political activity at the municipal, provincial
and federal levels, and by visible activities aimed deliber-
ately at evoking and advertising their ethnic heritage.

The Belgian Club as such never officially supported a particular political party. When in 1944 the Club hall was rented to the Commonwealth Educational Club and it was later discovered that the hall had in fact been used for the nomination of a C.C.F. candidate for the federal election, it was specifically asserted that the Club had no connection with any political party. Later in the same year, moreover, the hall was rented to an individual for his election campaign, "providing no political issues will be discussed at this gathering!" The Club did, understandably, encourage members of the Belgian community to enter politics and its support at the municipal level was frequently more than merely implicit.

The Club was also actively involved with defending the reputation of the Belgians. In 1928 Bishop Lloyd of Saskatoon wrote a series of letters to the *Manitoba Free Press*. The Bishop had been instrumental in founding the National Association of Canada and was determined that Canada should remain a British nation. Referring to the government's railway agreement, he wrote:

> During the last two years and a half the agreement has been in force the railways have dumped into this country an alarming number of European undesirables. Belgians have jumped in 1927 to 2,149 ... If the use of this has done so much harm to the blood of this country in the last two and a half years, the next two and a half years will be much more harmful ... But this railway agreement is flooding the country with undesirable Europeans by tens of thousands and the vitiation of the blood and character of this as a British nation can never be rectified.

Not surprisingly, Bishop Lloyd's statement drew some

adverse criticisms. One reader, signing himself 'A Canadian', questioned, "Is it proper for a minister of the Gospel to call people from Germany, Austria and other countries mongrels, dirty, etc.?", and also pointed out that "some of the British harvesters when they come here think Canada owes them a living." Undaunted by this, the Bishop returned to the attack:

> It is far better to get Old Country Britishers and teach them agriculture than fill the country with this Continental flood and try to civilize them ... No matter how much mud they sling at me, I am determined, as far as it lies in my power, that this country shall remain British and a part of the British Empire.

Although this slur was aimed at many groups, the Belgians had specifically been included, and the Club immediately enlisted the aid of the Belgian consul in drafting a suitable reply and letter of protest. Their indignation must quickly have subsided, however, as no such letter was ever published.

A more positive reaction to prejudice lay in continued participation in community and particularly patriotic activities. The annual Armistice Day ceremonies served to remind other Manitobans of the losses suffered by the Belgian Canadians during the First World War. A monument to the fallen, sculptured by Hubert Garnier, was unveiled on Provencher Boulevard directly in front of the Belgian Club in 1938 by Baron Silvercruys, the Belgian minister to Canada.

During the Second World War many young Belgians in Manitoba again served in the Canadian army, and understandably the partial liberation of Belgium in 1944 was suitably celebrated. The *Winnipeg Tribune* reported:

> Winnipeg and vicinity Belgians celebrated Sunday morning for the partial liberation of Belgium. They met at the Belgian Club on Provencher Avenue, and with flags waving and band playing, proceeded to the Belgian Sacred Heart Church on Plinquet Avenue, where Te Deum mass was sung by Father Peter ... Father Peter gave his address in the three languages. After mass, the celebrants returned to the cenotaph on Provencher Avenue where a prayer was said and the Last Post sounded.

From the very beginning the Belgian community took steps to advertise its ethnic heritage, although these steps were often halting or infrequent, and were complicated by attempts to define 'Belgians' when so many were intermarrying with other ethnic groups. At first the ethnic heritage was presented through participation in annual celebrations and in occasional advertising of events in local and Detroit newspapers. Later, however, there was a more determined and serious attempt to establish self-identity and to appeal for representation in the Canadian Senate. Most recently, the search for ethnic identity has been bolstered by participation in national ethnic conferences, by visits from the Flemish parliamentary cultural delegation, and by the formation of a club to promote more actively the annual Kermis Festival.

The Belgian Club, despite its shortcomings and periodic financial problems, has served as a focus of the activities and interests of the Belgian community in Manitoba. If it can justifiably be criticised for a certain lack of interest in cultural affairs, it is because it has always reflected the general attitudes of the Belgian community. Moreover, its leadership potential has been weakened by its failure to attract or retain active membership from the professions. Any ethnic club, such as the Belgian Club, exists to serve the needs of the majority of its members, and while at times its leaders could have taken a broader perspective, they could in effect act only with the support of the general membership.

While the Club can claim success in many of its endeavours, it must admit failure in making known the Belgian community to the people of Manitoba many of whom are still unaware of their fellow citizens of Belgian origin. While individuals may be known, the group as an entity is certainly not. Only a specific and determined effort will ensure that the attributes and contributions of the Belgians to the development and cultural mosaic of Manitoba will receive their deserved recognition.

CHAPTER IV

Religion, Education and Cultural Activities

TRADITIONALLY all Belgians have been Roman Catholics who have taken for granted the close inter-relationship of religion, education and certain aspects of their culture. The Flemings and the Walloons have, however, tended to differ in that the former have been regarded as more conservative and strict in their religious observances than the latter. These differing attitudes, paralleling their ethnic and linguisitic differences, were reflected in the Belgian immigrants who came to Manitoba.

As many Belgians settled initially in St. Boniface, the French-speaking Walloons tended to merge readily with the French population whose religious life was centred on St. Boniface Cathedral.

At first, this was true also of the Flemings for whose use Archbishop Beliveau designated a chapel at the Cathedral. In this chapel, Sunday morning mass was said in Flemish, and on Sunday afternoons catechism instruction was given in Flemish by two missionaries, Fathers De Munter and Van Den Bossche. As early as 1914 the Belgian Club discussed the possible establishment of a distinctively Flemish church, and as the nucleus of a separate parish already existed, it was not long before their hopes were realized.

49

In 1916 Father Kwakman was appointed pastor to this flock and he proceeded rapidly with the organization of a Belgian parish and with plans to build a church. By the following year the church had been erected and the parish incorporated. The canonical decree of establishment, translated from the original French, reads as follows:

> Canonical Decree of Establishment of the Catholic Parish of the Sacred Heart of St. Boniface.
>
> Arthur Beliveau, D.D., by the grace of God and the grace of the Holy Apostolic See, Archbishop of St. Boniface.
>
> To all who see these presents, take notice that by these presents We recognize and erect as a Catholic parish for the service of the faithful of the Flemish language of the parish of St. Boniface, under the name of "The Catholic Parish of the Sacred Heart of St. Boniface" and under

HERRINNERING AAN DE WYDING DER EERSTE BELGISCHE KERK IN MANITOBA. 7 OCTOBER 1917

SOUVENIR DE BÉNÉDICTION DE LA PREMIÈRE EGLISE BELGE AU MANITOBA. 7 OCTOBRE 1917

The Belgian Sacred Heart Church, 1917

the invocation of the Sacred Heart, the same
territory as that of the parish of St. Boniface.

To be the said Catholic parish, "The Catholic
Parish of the Sacred Heart of St. Boniface," en-
tirely under Our jurisdiction, in the care of the
pastors or ministers which We or Our successors
decide to appoint, to conform in everything to
the ecclesiastical disciplinary rules established in
this diocese, especially, to administer the sacra-
ments, preach the word of God, and to give the
other comforts of the holy religion to the faithful
of the said parish; in addition to these, to render
respect and obedience to the said pastors or ministers and to assist in the propagation of the faith
and the upkeep of the said pastors or ministers.

The said Catholic parish, "The Catholic Parish
of the Sacred Heart of St. Boniface," is, by these
presents, canonically established and becomes a
political, incorporated body. And by the unique
fact of the present decree, the said Catholic
parish, "The Catholic Parish of the Sacred Heart
of St. Boniface," becomes a Civil Corporation by
virtue of Chapter XXIII of the Statutes of Manitoba, 38 Victoria (22 July 1874).

The present decree shall be read and proclaimed
from the pulpit at the first community mass held
in the said parish after receipt of said decree.

Given at St. Boniface, under Our signature, the
seal of the diocese and the counter-signature of
Our chancellor, the ninth day of the month of
October, 1917.

Arthur, Archbishop of St. Boniface.

J. H. Prud'homme, Chancellor.

Father Kwakman, a Dutch priest, was the first pastor
of the Sacred Heart parish. He worked closely with the
Belgian Club, and, being interested in the economic as well
as the spiritual welfare of his parishioners, fully supported
such organizations as the Belgian Ladies Sick Visiting
Society although he had apparently not been consulted

prior to its formation in 1926. Father Kwakman similarly threw his wholehearted support behind the organization of the Belgian Mutual Benefit Society two years later. But although he won both moral and financial support from the Belgian Club, he faced continual difficulties in building his congregation.

Later in 1928 Father Kwakman was transferred to Qu'Appelle, Saskatchewan, and the Capuchins were invited to take over the parish. The Capuchins were a branch of the Franciscans who had been reorganized in the nineteenth century into three distinct orders: the Friars Minor, the Friars Minor Capuchin and the Friars Minor Conventual. The Capuchins had worked in Acadia during the French regime, but they returned to France in 1654. During the next two decades individual Capuchins worked in Canada, but they did not return as a group until 1890, when they settled in Ottawa. Other Capuchins, largely from Belgium and Holland, came individually or in small groups to minister to Flemish and Dutch settlers in Ontario and the prairie provinces. The Belgian Capuchins in Manitoba are now part of the Vice-Province of Central Canada. Their Superior in Orangeville, Ontario, is responsible for parish appointments subject to the approval of the appropriate archbishop.

The Capuchins' Provincial in Belgium in 1928 was Father Chrysostom, and it was he, apparently, who petitioned Archbishop Beliveau for permission to establish members of his order in the St. Boniface area. On receipt of the Archbishop's reply that the Flemish parish of the Sacred Heart was at their disposal, the Capuchins accepted the offer and Father Chrysostom came to St. Boniface as parish priest, local Superior and as Superior General of the Belgian Capuchins in Canada.

Instructing Father Willibrord from Blenheim, Ontario, to take up permanent residence in St. Boniface to await his arrival and that of a Capuchin Brother, Father Chrysostom left Antwerp for Canada in October 1928. The following excerpts from his diary provide a vivid picture of life in Manitoba as it appeared to this priestly newcomer, and of his attempts to help his parishioners:

October 10, 1928. Sailed from Antwerp with Brother Marius, made an official visit to Blenheim where I left Brother Marius and brought Brother Mensuetus along to St. Boniface, where we arrived in the forenoon of October 30, 1928. We are thus put in charge here of the Belgian parish of the Sacred Heart. All Flemish and Netherlands speaking people of St. Boniface and St. Vital are our parishioners, no matter where they live. The parish divisions here are linguistic, thus, Walloons, although they are Belgians, are not our parishioners but belong to the French parish of the Cathedral. Here, Belgian means a Fleming and speaking Belgian means speaking Flemish. Houses and church are built of wooden boards, everything seems poor, cheap and very small. Religious and spiritual conditions are even poorer. Worse than imaginable as experience has taught us.

November 29, 1928. Bought a car today, a Chrysler, something one can hardly do without in this country.

December 31, 1928. Personally handed over copies of baptismal and marriage certificates to the secretary of the diocese. Our parish is still over $9,000.00 in debt. So ends the year with the coldest day experienced so far.

January 6, 1929. Started to organize parochial societies in order to generate more community involvement in the parish — nothing of this nature existed here.

Established an Altar Society for the ladies who want to cooperate in whatever manner for the benefit of the church: renovation, decoration, etc. Managed to get 17 ladies together and they have begun by holding a sewing bee one afternoon per week in our all too small parsonage.

January 16, 1929. Founded a Propaganda Legion for the men to promote and spread good in the parish. To this end I have ordered first 100 and later 250 copies of the Catholic paper *De Ster* from Antwerp which are arriving regularly and are distributed free at Sunday masses. The Propaganda Legion hasn't accomplished much.

January 20, 1929. Founded the Eucharistic Crusaders for the children (Boys and girls) of the catechism classes and ordered 100 beautiful badges from Belgium.

January 27, 1929. Started a library with an initial order of Flemish books from Belgium (3000 francs worth) which Father Peter brought with him.

February 10, 1929. Organized card parties which will be held every second Sunday evening in the chapel hall. Initial attendance very good (about 100). These card parties are run by the Altar Society with the profit going to the church. In this manner some semblance of community cooperation and activity has been brought into our parish.

October 14, 1929. Wrote to the convent of Leeuwen-Heverlee in Belgium to persuade these sisters to come and establish themselves in our midst. No luck there.

November 27, 1929. Following negotiations with Archbishop Sinnott of Winnipeg, Father Emmanuel and Brother Angelmus leave our parish to take over the parish of Plumas, Manitoba, on a permanent basis.

February 8, 1930. At the request of the Executive of the Belgian Club, classes in the Flemish language were initiated. These were held Saturday afternoons, starting with 40 students and soon increasing to 50 students, between the ages of 6 to 19 years.

March 1, 1930. Mailed 355 Flemish and 100 French letters of appeal to our benefactors in Belgium, asking for help to build a kindergarten and cloister in our parish.

March 25, 1930. Started mailing sealed invitations to non-practising parishioners to fulfill their Easter duties and attend mass on Sundays.

September 15, 1930. Flemish language classes suspended due to dwindled interest. It wasn't worth the effort.

February, 1931. Tried to establish a Flemish language weekly paper. Could find little support, so nothing developed.

March 13, 1931. During the night a huge cross was erected behind our grounds. By whom and for what purpose? People think that it's a warning from the Ku Klux Klan that they will put everything to the torch! May God protect us.

July 19, 1931. On the occasion of Belgian Independence Day, blessed a banner of the Belgian Veterans' Association in Canada.

September, 1931. We started taking lessons in the English language.

May 5, 1933. Received verbal consent from Monsignor Jubinville, Administrator of the diocese, to erect a building (at our own expense) on Springfield (now Dugald) Road for the purpose of teaching catechism and celebrating mass on Sundays. (This was named St. Francis Church and is still maintained by the Capuchins).

February 22, 1934. A Solemn State Memorial Service was held in our Belgian Sacred Heart church in honour of King Albert I of the Belgians. Notables present included Archbishop Monsignor Beliveau, Monsignor Chevrier, Chief Justice Prendergast representing the King of England, Premier Bracken of Manitoba, Mayor Turner, General Beeman, all the Consuls based in Winnipeg etc. I performed the service and rendered the eulogy in both Flemish and French, Belgium's two offi-

cial languages. The Princess Patricia military
band was in attendance, and played several
beautiful and appropriate pieces. Everything
turned out well.

The formation of the sub-parish of St. Francis in 1933
is worthy of note as it represented a special effort by Father
Chrysostom to improve social and spiritual conditions
among the Belgians who lived in the area of the St. Boniface
city dump. With some initial Protestant help, Father Chrysostom began a series of social and recreational activities
centred at the church. These later became associated with
the local community club.

A few months later, Father Chrysostom left the parish
and was replaced by Father Damas. Father Damas' first
impression of St. Boniface was that it was "primitive and
quite different from the old country," but he nevertheless
threw himself wholeheartedly into his parochial work. He

Grotto of Our Lady of Lourdes

was an enthusiastic builder who in a mere three years completely transformed the appearance of the church, presbytery, chapel, cemetery and grounds while at the same time building on the banks of the Seine River the grotto Our Lady of Lourdes, an exact replica of the world famous shrine of Notre Dame de Lourdes in France. This shrine became famous throughout North America as a tourist attraction and a place of pilgrimage.

Father Damas left a vivid description of the opening of the shrine:

> The official opening and blessing of our grotto was held in the afternoon of Sunday, May 25, 1936, in the presence of a crowd estimated at between five to six thousand people, many non-Catholics, several Protestant ministers and many out-of-town visitors. Conspicuously absent were several Catholic clergymen who had been sent written invitations. Co-adjutor Archbishop, His Excellency Monsignor Yelle, was officially received and led in procession to the grotto. The La Vérendrye Band was in attendance and led the procession, followed by all the parochial banners and the faithful. The ceremony itself took place on the grotto grounds. The dedication was given by Father Damas in Flemish, French and English. The sermons were preached by Monsignor Jubinville, pastor of the Cathedral, in French, Rev. Father E. H. Brodeau, pastor of Holy Cross parish, in English and Very Rev. Father Chrysostom in Flemish. His Excellency Monsignor Yelle also gave an address. Lunch and refreshments were served in the parish hall. In the evening a solemn candle-light procession was held in the presence of a crowd numbering between four and five thousand people. It was decided to hold a candle-light procession every third Sunday of the summer months from May

to September. The entire parish co-operated to
the fullest to make this day a real success.

Father Damas' interests and energies extended far beyond
his regular parish duties and his building program. He was
also the driving force behind the formation of a Belgian
Credit Union in 1939.

He regarded his duties as encompassing both the material
and the spiritual well-being of his flock, and although the
time seemed ill-chosen, he became convinced of the benefit
to his parishioners of a credit union. Very few Belgians
had even heard of a credit union, and the traditional reluc-
tance of Belgians to venture into new financial enterprises
hardly boded well. The purpose of a credit union was
essentially four-fold:

> 1) to teach and encourage the habit of thrift by
>   providing a safe, convenient and attractive
>   medium for the investment of the savings of its
>   members;
>
> 2) to help members handle their own finances and
>   to encourage them to live within their means;
>
> 3) to eliminate usury, establish productive credit,
>   and increase the purchasing power of its members
>   by enabling them to borrow for productive and
>   provident purposes at a reasonable rate of inter-
>   est;
>
> 4) to train its members in sound business methods
>   and self-government and bring them to a full
>   realization of the value of co-operation.

After several delays, a meeting was called on January
9, 1939. Of the 70 parishioners invited, only 30 attended.

These all received copies of "A Manitoba Credit Union Catechism" in order to familiarize them with the purposes and function of credit unions. At the same inaugural meeting, a provisional board of directors was nominated. The five members included Father Damas. Attendance at the second meeting dwindled to 20, and to 15 at the third meeting. Even this did not deter Father Damas, and at the fourth meeting, when attendance again increased slightly, a regular committee was elected. It was unanimously decided to adopt the name "Belgian Sacred Heart's Credit Union Society," and shortly afterwards, through the untiring efforts of Father Damas and increasing support of the dairy farmers and the parishioners of Holy Cross in Norwood, sufficient deposits were secured to enable the first loan to be made. Confidence was gradually built-up, and the number of deposits and loans increased.

In 1941 Father Damas was transferred to another mission and was replaced by Father Peter who, having served the parish for a number of years, was already well acquainted with his parishioners. He continued the leadership of Father Damas and the Credit Union gained further strength. In 1951 the Belgian Club invested some of its surplus funds in the Credit Union, and this practice has since continued. Today the Credit Union, since 1974 officially called the Belgian Credit Union, is a fitting tribute to the pioneer efforts of Father Damas, and its benefits have long been extended beyond the Belgian community.

Traditionally, the church has served several functions besides the spiritual. The Credit Union is but one example of pastoral concern with the material interests of the parishioners, but the church also served social needs through the establishment of such organizations as community clubs, ladies groups, boy scouts and girl guides, and through fairly close cooperation with the Belgian Club. It is understandable, then, that the Belgians took pride in their church leaders. The appointment of Father Remi De Roo as bishop of Victoria, B.C. in 1962 brought a congratulatory letter from the Belgian Club:

> We are most happy and justly proud of your elevation in the hierarchy of the church. We deem it a great honor indeed, and an unusual distinction that a son of one of our earliest Belgian pioneers in Manitoba has been elevated to the high rank you will soon be occupying in the Catholic Church.

A similar congratulation went to Father Antoine Hacault on his appointment as auxiliary bishop of St. Boniface in 1964; while the Belgian origin of Archbishop Baudoux of St. Boniface was a source of constant pride.

As has been seen, the Sacred Heart parish was the only Catholic parish in Manitoba to be officially designated as Flemish. But members of the Capuchin order and other Flemish and Walloon priests served in many of the parishes throughout the province especially but not exclusively where there were sizeable Belgian settlements. St. Hyacinth parish at Portage la Prairie was entrusted to the Capuchins in 1952, Sacred Heart parish at Roblin in 1972, and Saint Mary's parish at Souris in 1973. Belgian priests also served at St. Alphonse, Swan Lake, Ste. Rose-du-Lac, Deloraine, and Bruxelles where a Belgian Ursuline convent was built in 1916. In many of these rural parishes, the first masses were said in Flemish, but as the population moved or integrated, the English language gradually became predominant. In all these parishes, the church served as a focal point of community life and of ethnic pride. The 75th anniversary of Belgian Independence, for example, was celebrated with great verve in Holland and Bruxelles, but the celebrations centred around the church. In all the smaller Belgian communities the priests were in a very real sense community leaders.

In most of these small towns, however, there was a gradual tendency for the focus of community activities to move from the churches to local clubs.

Although many of the Belgian immigrants to Manitoba were not themselves well educated, education gradually became a greater interest. There was early concern for their own language and its support either through the public school system or through libraries and special classes.

Only one year after the foundation of the Belgian Club the Executive passed a motion requesting a Flemish school in St. Boniface. Following the controversy known as the Manitoba Schools Question, the provincial government in 1897 amended the law by adopting the bilingual clause:

> Where ten of the pupils in any school speak the French language (or any language other than English) as their native language, the teaching of such pupils shall be conducted in French (or such other language), and English upon the bilingual system.

Invoking this clause, in 1906 the Belgian settlers living near the Seine River petitioned the St. Boniface school board for the provision of instruction in Flemish. The Board asked the Marian Brotherhood to find a teacher capable of providing this instruction, but as they were unable to do so, the petition was denied. There is no record of similar petitions in any of the smaller Belgian settlements in Manitoba.

The bilingual system of education established in 1897 gradually became a multilingual system, and weaknesses soon became apparent. These weaknesses were sufficient excuse for the new provincial government of Premier Norris to abolish the system in 1916. From this time on, English was to be the only legal language of instruction in the public schools. This action, as has been seen, brought from the Belgian Club an expression of support for the M.L.A. for Ste. Rose-du-Lac who had opposed the legislation, but the issue seems to have been carried no further.

As the public schools could not be used to safeguard the Flemish language, the Belgians depended more on two other means. The original charter of the Belgian Club had included the formation and maintenance of a library among the purposes of the Club. Accordingly a reading room was immediately provided and subscriptions to several newspapers were taken out.

For some reason, the concept of a reading room and library did not win continuing support, and by 1928 an attempt was begun to revive it. In the following year a visiting professor from Ghent promised to contact the Belgian government and seek its help in establishing a library at the Club, while at the same time Father Chrysostom reported the formation of a small library of Flemish books many of which had been brought by Father Peter. After this time, intermittent attempts were made to provide Flemish reading material, but the reading room and library at the Club have never assumed the importance they deserve.

Several specific attempts have been made over the years to provide instruction in the Flemish language. In 1926 the Belgian Club began weekly classes in Flemish, but they cannot have long continued for in 1930, at the Club's request, Father Chrysostom initiated similar classes. Again, lack of interest led to their cancellation within a year. From that time, little more was done until recent years. In 1973 another attempt was made, and currently a small class is being held. It seems doubtful, however, whether there is sufficient latent interest to revive the Flemish language among the younger generation of Belgians in Manitoba.

While the Belgians have made little concerted attempt to maintain the Flemish language, they have shown an ever increasing degree of support for education itself, and especially for the further education of their own group. This has taken the form of both moral and financial support.

Interest in formal education, beyond what was required by law, was slow in developing; but by the 1920's the Belgians had become more aware of the value of education. Thus in 1920 Brothers of the Order of the Sacred Heart were encouraged to open a boarding school for boys in Swan Lake. The school flourished for several years, enrolling at one time as many as 100 boarders and many more in a day school. The numbers gradually decreased, however, and the school was closed in 1932. The Belgians had also begun to take pride in the achievements of individual Belgians. In 1922, for example, the Club approved a memorial project for L. Vankoughnet who, as deputy

superintendent-general for the Department of Indian
Affairs in the 1880's, had been largely responsible for the
establishment of the first three Indian industrial schools
in western Canada. The Club frequently congratulated
young Belgians who had won scholastic awards, and in
1941 it decided to provide a fund to support the further
education of young Belgians on a systematic basis. These
intentions were not immediately put into action, however,
and it was not till ten years later that a definite decision
was made to provide regular scholarships. Initially, funds
provided only two $50 scholarships, one for a son and one
for a daughter of a Club member. Once the precedent had
been established, however, the practice gained more support. By 1954 the annual awards totalled $400, and in 1962
the quota was considerably increased although the following proviso was added:

> ...should the recipients of scholarships attain
> prominence in business or professions, they
> voluntarily return the amount of the bursary to
> the Club so that it may be added to the regular
> quota, thus increasing the total value of the
> annual grants.

In 1967 the first such refund was made, and the annual
scholarships were acknowledged to be a worthwhile undertaking. The practice of presenting the awards at a Club
meeting addressed by a prominent educator brought further
support and publicity. The awards have since 1971 been
open to "any student of Belgian heritage in the community." These awards, and the scholarships given annually
by the Ladies Auxiliary, Belgian Veterans' Association, for
students entering Grade XI, continue to demonstrate the

importance which the Club attaches to the support of education.

From the early years, the Belgian immigrants maintained a considerable interest in cultural activities, especially in music and drama.

The Belgian interest in music centred largely on bands. This form of music in the Canadian West dated back to 1866 when Abbé Georges Dugas of St. Boniface College formed a small band, and a succession of others kept the tradition alive until 1910-1912 when two distinct bands were formed. These were the St. Boniface City Band, commonly known as the Belgian Band, and the La Vérendrye Band which, though essentially French, was founded by a Belgian, Joseph Vermander.

The Belgian Band gave regular concerts at the Club and two special concerts each year: on New Year's Day and

The Bruxelles Band

on the Saturday closest to July 21, the Belgian Independence Day. Moreover, the Band participated in special events and parades. Like all similar organizations, the Band experienced occasional difficulties, but in 1944 it was reorganized and, after an unsuccessful attempt to amalgamate with the La Vérendrye Band, it began to flourish. Continued support from the Club and a grant from the city have enabled the Band to continue, so that today, with a membership which is now largely non-Belgian, it still maintains a high musical standard.

The main interest of the Belgians remained in band music, both in St. Boniface and in several of the smaller towns such as Bruxelles, Deloraine, and Ste. Rose-du-Lac. In Holland there was a brass band organized as early as 1894, and although it was dissolved by 1900, it was later revived for 13 years from 1949 to 1962. Similarly, Belgians

Belgica Dramatic Club patriotic pageant, 1916

were active in a band at Ste. Rose-du-Lac from 1904 onwards and in Bruxelles where the band still exists. Bruxelles could reasonably have claimed to be the musical capital of rural Manitoba, for at one time it boasted four orchestras in addition to the band.

Belgians, and particularly the Belgian Club, also took pride in the musical accomplishments of individual Belgians such as Albert Simoens and others who performed outstandingly in musical competitions. Choral music was largely confined to the various church choirs, although the choir of the dramatic club 'Excelsior' was active during the 1940's when it made several broadcasts.

Along with music, the Belgians were actively interested in drama. As early as 1916 a theatre group, known as the 'Onder Ons' was established; and this was followed a little later by the formation of the 'Belgica' group which staged plays for Belgian war relief. The 'Excelsior' group existed during the early 1940's; while in more recent years some financial support has been extended to non-Belgian groups such as the Cercle Molière in St. Boniface.

During the many years since Belgians first came to Manitoba and since the formation of the Belgian Club, the Belgian community has changed in many ways, as new generations of Belgians born in Manitoba have grown up and adopted many aspects of the predominant culture. Yet some things remain the same. The Sacred Heart parish is still officially and emotionally the parish of the Belgians, and the musical traditions of the Belgians are still continued. Educationally, the Belgians have achieved well, but frequently at the expense of their traditional language. Although it may well be that the Belgians in Manitoba form too small a group to maintain effectively their ethnic consciousness, there can be little doubt that many younger Belgians still yearn for some more tangible link with their cultural heritage. All individuals are creatures of their past, whether they realize it or not, and it may be that only a more determined effort to revive cultural traditions will enable the Belgians of today to regain a full and confident pride in their distinctive ethnic character.

CHAPTER V

Occupations

ALTHOUGH Belgian immigrants to Manitoba have engaged in a variety of occupations, their main interests have been in farming and construction.

As the first immigrants came mainly from over-populated villages in Belgium, they naturally tended to become farmers when they arrived in Manitoba. The majority of these took up mixed farming in the areas around St. Alphonse, Mariapolis, Swan Lake and Deloraine, while some became dairy farmers around Winnipeg.

Those engaged in mixed farming soon earned respect for their industry, and as many of them were financially solvent, it was not long before substantial farms were acquired. One pioneer Belgian farmer recalled that within a year and a half:

> J'ai construit une maison, étable et grainerie, et j'ai achêté deux chevaux, une vache, un veau, une charrue, une voiture, et un traineau pour faire les transports en hiver, 3 cochons, deux douzaines de poules. J'ai mis en culture la première année 12 acres; j'ai fait du labour pour l'année prochaine, 20 acres prêtes à semer, en tout 32 acres.

On the other hand, several Belgian farmers arrived here

penniless. Through hard work, thrift even beyond the belief of many Scots, and through willingness to accept all types of jobs, many of these were able gradually to own their own homesteads. A settler wrote:

> Maurice cleared bush for the family for three months at $35.00 per month, then in July he was hired for the harvest by another family for $45.00 per month. He stayed there the following winter for board and tobacco money. He stayed at the farm for five years until 1916, then purchased a local homestead including livestock, equipment and household for $5,000.00.

These farmers were understandably pleased with their gains in Manitoba and, as has been seen, their letters home encouraged many of their friends and relatives to join them. Conditions, of course, were not necessarily at first any easier for many of the immigrants who arrived later after the First World War. One such immigrant has left a graphic account of events following his arrival in Winnipeg in 1927.

> I was so happy and relieved to hear strangers speaking the Belgian language. The strangers were Belgian landlords of Belgian farmers. One farmer gave me a job for fifty dollars a month. The twelve immigrants from Belgium had to separate and take jobs at different places. We shook hands and promised to see each other again some day. I found myself wondering what kind of a position I would have and if the job would be hard and what kind of a job was waiting for me. I found out the next day. I worked for a dairy farmer, got up at 4 o'clock in the morning, warmed the furnace for hot water, and worked hard for the rest of the day. I couldn't milk cows very well, so in June 1927, I began to work in the hayfield. That was the hardest work of all.

We pitched hay for fourteen hours a day, with a fork, but without gloves. I got eleven blisters on my hands. I got a needle and thread to puncture the blisters and drain them. The next day I got a pair of gloves and continued working there for a month. Then I quit. I received a letter from a friend in Alberta who said he was making six to eight dollars a day, unloading rails and ties. I wanted those kind of wages too. The farmer told me that if I would stay he would pay me seventy-five dollars a month, and that I could work for him in the winter also, cleaning and feeding cows for twenty-five dollars a month. But my mind was already made up. I wanted to travel and make more money. I found out later that this was the wrong kind of thinking for me. I arrived at my friend's in Glendoland, Alberta and started working the next day. The work was very hard and tiresome, but I had to keep on going as I had no money or home. It was an obligation. So after cursing and feeling sorry for myself, I went through that painful job for two months, finished, and returned by train to Winnipeg. At the station in Saskatoon, I had to wait an hour. In the meantime a farmer asked me if I had work. I said no and he told me he needed six men to help harvest in Hanley. The farmer's name was McKenzie. The pay was seven dollars a day, which was high for those times. The meals were excellent. But we had no luck, because after eight days work it started raining and a few days after that it began to snow and freeze. The farmer told us there would be no more threshing for a long time. He took me to the station, said good-bye and I came back to Winnipeg. It was already the end of October in 1927. I took it easy for a few days, then took a job digging sewers for thirty-seven and a half cents an hour. Then after four weeks I finished, with very little money left. In December 1927 men were needed to clear bush from Cranberry Portage to Flin Flon, for a new railroad. Twelve of us Belgian greenhorns, all inexperienced bushworkers, took a half mile bush clearing job, cutting those big trees and burning them. We slept in tents and ate in the bunkhouse. We slept on brush and hay on the floor. It was very cold, almost 40 below practically everyday. We spent three weeks there, sleeping with all our clothes on, just taking off our boots at night. In Europe there is never any ice in the bedrooms from the cold, but in spite of all the blankets we used here, there was frost in the morning at the hole we left for breathing. After three weeks, the half mile was finished, but to our surprise each of us was seventy dollars in the hole. We had worked so hard and looked like devils from the smoke, so the boss felt sorry for us and gave us another half mile to do. This time it was all swampy with only small trees and brush. We were finished in one day. We went to The Pas, got rooms in the hotel and spent the money. It was now January, 1928. We split up, six of us going to Winnipeg and six of us went back on the railway line. This time the job paid thirty-five cents an hour with a ten hour day. Board and

Belgians working on the railway

room cost seventy-five cents a day, in March 1928. We came back on a flatcar from Cranberry Portage in temperatures of twenty below. I got to The Pas half frozen. In the hotel room, I nursed my stiff legs from the frost by rubbing them with alcohol. In a couple of days, I had normal blood circulation. In April, a Belgian contractor came to The Pas with about two hundred workers, all for the new railroad from Nelson to Churchill, called the Hudson Bay Line. We were divided into groups of four and boarded the train for Nelson. That's as far as the train went. We walked the rest of the way. Four of us with our heavy packsacks walked seventy-two miles through muskeg and snow.

It was still very cold those three and a half days. Every twenty miles there was a cache or store-house. We ate and slept there over night and then went on our way. It was now halfway through April and still there was lots of snow. When we came to our post, there was a whole pile of supplies covered with a tent. The items had been freighted in by tractor and sled. There were four wheelbarrows, two saws, two hammers, a bag of nails, two rolls of tarpaper, a tin stove with an oven, a coal oil lamp, blankets, axes, shovels, sugar, flour, oatmeal, lard, butter, dry beans, coffee, tea, dry milk, salt pork and hay for bedding. We busied ourselves shovelling snow, and putting up the tent. The next day we cut trees to make the frame for our castle. We nailed poles together, and put tarpaper over the frame. We made beds, four in a row with small poles, and put cheesecloth around them, so the mosqui-toes wouldn't eat us alive. We added the brush and the hay and our beds were ready. We had a few boards to make a door and a table, and a couple of boxes made chairs. Then we began our task of cutting trees and clearing the half mile for the tracks. It was June before the snow was gone and we could start digging and wheeling the dirt, which we piled almost six feet high in places, to put the railway tracks on. I was the baker and cook. Sunday was my baking day. We got dry yeast and made about twenty-four loaves of bread for the week. The others collected dry wood for the week. That was our Sunday pastime. The menu for breakfast was porridge, pancakes, bread, jam, coffee; for dinner, boiled pork and beans, powdered eggs, bread, jam and coffee; for supper, pork and beans, bread, jam, dry fruit cooked, tea. It was truly a wilderness, with swamps, muskeg, millions of insects, isolation of hundreds of miles from towns, hard and tiresome work, sometimes in water and mud up to the knees. After six months or so the hardship could be easily forgotten because the pay was good. This continued from 1928 until the end of October 1929. Some of the men stayed during the winter to lay the tracks to Churchill, but most of us came to Winnipeg to whoop it up and forget the hard times. You could spend your money much faster than you could make it. In November I got on a trip to Belgium for four months and then returned the end of March 1929. In April I got back on the Hudson Bay line. No walking this time as the rails were laid all the way to Churchill, and a truck on rails brought us there. We began the same routine. This time, we only made ditches for a half mile alongside the tracks, clear the brush one hundred feet wide, make off track ditches, and dynamite dams made by the beavers. We had the same menu for the entire six months.

During that time, there was one incident that I shall never forget. On the way to the Hudson Bay line in August 1929, one beautiful, sun shiny Sunday morning when the birds were singing in the trees, I felt very happy and decided to take a walk. I walked along the railroad tracks for a half mile to the neighbouring group of workers. I was whistling a tune about halfway there when it happened. I looked sideways into the bush and to my surprise, there was a big silver haired polar bear staring at me about twenty-five feet away.

My whistle froze. I could feel the hair standing
on end on my head. It was as though I was
paralyzed. Automatically, I started running as
fast as I could, looking over my shoulder at the
same time. I'm sure a jack rabbit couldn't outrun
me that time. I was so exhausted, I nearly
dropped. The bear was later shot farther up the
line. He weighed nine hundred pounds. That was
the only bear I've seen that close outside of a
zoo.
We arrived at Churchill the end of October 1929
... We returned to Winnipeg later in the year,
and celebrated to forget the miserable life we had
just left, and the Hudson Bay line.

As mixed farmers, Belgian immigrants introduced new
types of husbandry to Manitoba. In particular, they introduced two new breeds of horse: the Belgian and Percheron. The first Belgian horse, Napoleon, was owned by
the Lombaert brothers of St. Alphonse; the first Percheron,
Charlotte, was owned by a syndicate in Swan Lake and
was later sold to a Winnipeg firm for a handsome profit.

These two types of horse were fairly similar. Both were
originally bred for size, first for knights during the Middle
Ages and later as draft horses. Their size made them excep-
tionally well suited for agricultural work. The Belgian,
chestnut brown in colour and bred in the Low Countries,
was generally docile and patient; the Percheron, grey or
black in colour and bred in La Perche, Normandy, was
exceedingly active and nimble. Because both types of horse
were in great demand both for their special qualities and
for their investment value, many Belgian farmers began
horse breeding and developed strains which compared favourably with those of Belgium and France.

The federal and provincial governments were quick to

realize the value of this type of husbandry, and to provide encouragement and assistance through the establishment of local clubs. Members of each club guaranteed a certain number of mares to be bred to an approved stallion, while the owner agreed to restrict the use of the stallion, at a stated service fee, to the members of the club. The federal Department of Agriculture gave financial assistance depending on the membership of the club and on the number of mares in foal.

Although many Belgian farmers became involved in breeding horses both for their own use and for sale to Winnipeg business firms, the vast majority preferred the use of lighter and less expensive horses for farm work, especially when the average farmer might require anywhere from ten to eighteen horses.

After 1920 mechanization drastically reduced the need for horses on farms. Belgian farmers, progressive in farm operating methods, were quick to adapt to mechanization, a Belgian being the first farmer in the Deloraine district to obtain a tractor. Another Belgian, Van Ryssel, won international recognition for his work in developing a variety of flax.

In addition to mixed farming, Belgians also engaged in market gardening in both the urban and rural areas of the province. Like many other European groups, they introduced new strains of market garden produce. The Andries family in the Turtle Mountain district has been particularly successful in developing specialized varieties of currants, gooseberries, raspberries, and strawberries.

Many pioneer dairy farmers in the province were Belgians, some of whom went into the dairy business. In 1890, for example, Constant Bossuyt bought the Northwestern Dairy, the first dairy established in Winnipeg, and renamed it the Manitoba Dairy. Still owned by the same family, its location has altered several times and is now at Oak Bluff.

Because of the nature of large scale dairying, farmers must locate reasonably close to cities which provide the population to consume milk products, and in fertile areas which provide the lush pasture for dairy cattle. Thus, early Belgian dairymen found a highly profitable market for dairy products in Winnipeg and its suburbs, and were able to farm in the ideal pastureland of the Red River valley. The first dairies were located in Stonewall, the Kildonans, St. Boniface, St. Vital, Fort Garry and River Heights.

Belgians were the largest single group of dairymen in Winnipeg, but their operations were on a small scale by modern standards. With seldom more than 50 cows, the typical Belgian dairy farmer sold independently what he produced in milk, butter and cream. Each dairy used its

Bossuyt milk delivery, 1905

own tokens as means of exchange. One small dairy farmer
recalled:

> Each morning after milking time we would finish
> our breakfast, clean the barn, and then my father,
> starting on a small scale, would take milk from
> our dairy at Kingston Row across the Red River
> on a barge in summer. From there, he followed
> a trail through River Park into Osborne Street
> and into Winnipeg. He supplied the boarding
> houses and hotels with milk. In wintertime, he
> would go around and over the Norwood Bridge.

Although many small dairies supplied commercial
establishments, others engaged in home delivery. At first,
the farmers delivered "loose milk."

> We would load up the wagon with 8 quart cans
> of milk. When we arrived on a particular route
> we would take a milk can off the wagon and
> go door to door with the can. At each home,
> the can lid would come off, turned upside down,
> and then filled with a quart of milk; each lid
> held exactly one quart. The housewife would
> usually ask for a quart and a quart would be
> measured out. In winter, the inside of the lid
> would sometimes gather a thin coat of ice. When
> this happened, we would go in the kitchen, melt
> the ice with warm water to insure the exact
> amount of milk. Otherwise you heard about it!

This type of handling lasted about thirty years, for by the
1920's many customers demanded bottled milk as a more
sanitary method of delivery. As this increased costs of delivery, many Belgian dairymen discontinued milk delivery
in favour of production and shipping to larger dairies such
as Crescent, Modern, Standard and the St. Boniface
Creamery. Improved standards of cleanliness, and the

compulsory pasteurization of milk prompted by polio out-
breaks in the 1930's further increased costs and drove many
more of the smaller dairies out of business.

Urbanization and the retirement of the first generation
of Belgian dairyman also reduced the number of dairies.
When many Belgian dairymen reached retirement age in
the 1940's, their sons often chose not to continue in the
business. In other cases, the father simply preferred to sell
his business and retire with his money safely in the bank.
Not infrequently this trend often coincided with the expansion of the urban area into areas which previously had
been good farm land. Dairy farmers were tempted to sell
their land, and many did so. These factors, combined with
increased operating costs and more stringent sanitation
regulations, reduced the number of dairies from as many
as fifty at one time, to fewer than half a dozen today.

Another closely related aspect of farming was the grain
business. No longer in business, but once dealing in grain,
flour, cereals and feeds was Soubry Grain, the only Belgian
elevator in the Winnipeg area. Founded in 1928, and at
first employing Belgians, this elevator served the needs of
most Belgian farmers and dairymen. It was located on
Archibald Street in the heart of St. Boniface's old Belgian
town.

While many Belgians were engaged in some form of
agriculture, there has always been a small but significant
group involved in small commercial operations: bakers,
butchers, blacksmiths, florists, monument makers and store
keepers. There has, however, been a gradual decline in the
numbers of small businesses owned and operated by Bel-

gians, although the Van Belleghem family has remained highly competitive in the hotel business.

Construction was for many years next in importance to farming for the Belgians in Manitoba. At the turn of the century there were several Belgian owned construction companies in St. Boniface, and these built many of the Belgian homes and businesses in addition to the first Belgian Club and the Belgian Sacred Heart Church. These companies gradually extended their operations throughout Winnipeg, the province and, later, Saskatchewan and Alberta.

Many Belgian immigrant carpenters at first worked for one of the companies until they had saved sufficient money to work independently. The outstanding example was Gerard Baert who first arrived in 1928 and worked for

Belgian workers at the Marion brickyard

five years as a carpenter before establishing his own company. Baert Construction, which soon earned a reputation for efficiency and good workmanship, became one of the largest construction companies in the province by the 1950's and 1960's before going bankrupt in 1973. Today the only large Belgian contractor is Bockstael Construction.

While the most able and ambitious formed their own companies or operated their own businesses, the vast majority of Belgians in the urban area remained employees who were willing to accept any type of work when employment was hard to find. Only in more recent years, especially after the Second World War, have Belgians entered the professions in significant numbers.

In search of a better way of life, many Belgians emigrated to Manitoba and entered a variety of occupations, early becoming a significant group in dairying and construction. The decline of their former dominance may be attributed to several factors, not least of which was the traditional Belgian individuality which inhibited the development of large corporate enterprises able to compete successfully in modern industry and commerce.

CHAPTER VI

Social Life: Sports and Pastimes

IMMIGRANTS tend to bring with them many of the recreational activities which they enjoyed in their native land. These vary from hobbies and simple social gatherings to organized and competitive sports. Sometimes these activities flourish unchanged in their new environment, but more often they are influenced and modified by natural factors such as geography and climate or by social factors such as the gradual integration of the immigrants into a new and different culture. The national enthusiasm for sports in Belgium was wholeheartedly continued by the immigrants to Manitoba where the Belgian Club served as a focal point for both cultural and recreational activities.

Pigeon racing has long been a popular sport among Belgians. It originated in 1815, and initially the tumbler and smerle pigeons were used. By cross breeding these with the English carrier pigeon, the modern racing pigeon was developed by the 1860's. The average bird weighs about 18 ounces and is slightly smaller than the crow. It is also very fast, being able to attain speeds as high as 80 miles per hour. This speed ensures its safety from all predators except the sparrow hawk. The pigeons used today come in a variety of colours, but are bred for strength rather than for appearance. They have adapted well to the climatic conditions of Manitoba. Being extremely hardy, they can remain outside in a loft all year round so long as they are kept dry, and are regularly exercised. Although many of the pigeons are now bred in Manitoba, some of the finest are still imported from Belgium at prices often in excess of $5,000. Imported birds must be registered with the Department of Defence in Ottawa.

The rules of pigeon racing are fairly simple. On the day before a race, all owners take their pigeons to a designated point which, in Winnipeg, is usually the Belgian Club. There, each bird is assigned a number, and an appropriate tag is attached to the bird's leg. The pigeons are then taken to places of varying distance from home, usually between 50 and 500 miles away. At a given time in early morning, the birds are released simultaneously. They then fly home, guided by instinct, at an average speed of approximately 40 miles per hour. Being excellent navigators, the birds will quite often seek and take advantage of a tail wind. At home, the pigeon owner has a time clock; and as soon as his first pigeon returns to the loft, he removes the bird's number tag and punches the time clock. The bird with the best speed wins the race. The Belgian system of awards is still used, with a prize being allotted for every ten pigeons entered in the race. This differs from the English system in which only the first three to finish receive a prize.

Pigeon racing in Manitoba was first organized in 1917 by the St. Boniface Racing Pigeon Club which was later associated with the Belgian Club. The rapid growth of interest in the sport led to the formation of a second club, the Norwood Pigeon Flyers, in 1938. These two clubs in 1967 formed the Metro Winnipeg Racing Pigeon Association, although they each retained their separate identity.

Today, races take place every weekend from the middle of May to the middle of September. The direction of the races changes from west-east to south-north every five years. The longest race from the west took place from Banff to Winnipeg in 1924; the longest from the south was from Oklahoma to Winnipeg in 1935. Flights to the east of Winnipeg are restricted to 500 miles because of the navigational problems posed by Lake Superior.

The two biggest races of the season in Winnipeg are the Old Bird Race and the Young Bird Race. The former is about 500 miles long. The latter, in which only birds born during the current season may be entered, is the last race of the year and is approximately 250 miles long. The distance difference of these two races illustrates the cyclical nature of the racing season. The first race of the year is 50 miles, and each succeeding race is an additional 50 miles. The Old Bird Race, the most prestigious, takes place in July, and after this a new cycle begins for young birds. The cycle continues until the Young Bird Race in September.

There are today about 100 active pigeon racers in Manitoba, most of them in Winnipeg or Brandon. It is interesting to note, however, that only about 20% of them are of Belgian origin. Although pigeon racing has long been popular in countries other than Belgium, it is the Belgian form of the sport which predominates in Manitoba where steps are now being taken further to increase its popularity among all age groups.

Another distinctively Belgian sport still practised in Manitoba is pole archery. The pioneer Joseph Vermander, an enthusiastic sportsman, recalled the organization of 'popingai' or 'papejay' shooting clubs "which the French call 'tir à la perche' and the English translate somewhat inadequately 'pole shooting.'" The sport, no matter what its correct English name, was first practised informally at the home of Theophile Gelaude in St. Vital in the early 1920's, but the sport was more formally organized with the formation in 1926 of the St. Sebastian Archery Club. The archery grounds were in the area bounded by Archibald Street, Provencher Avenue, the Seine River and the CNR tracks. A club was also organized at Ste. Amélie, and inter-club competition started in the same year. The need for a governing body soon became apparent, and the Manitoba Archery Association was formed in 1928. This was later renamed the Manitoba Pole Archery Association.

The popularity of the sport and the need for further competition led to the formation in 1929 of a second club in Winnipeg, the Robin Hood Archery Club, and of the Ste. Rose Archery Club which in 1934 amalgamated with the Ste. Amélie Club. Regular tournaments took place between the three clubs, and the popularity of the sport later reached into Ontario, where the Dryden Merrymen Archery Club was formed in 1970.

Belgian archery is quite different from English archery which is practised around the world. Its only similarity to the English version is in the use of a bow. In Belgian pole archery a wooden or metal pole 100 feet high is set up. The base of the pole is weighted, and the pole is pinned to two posts. The balanced weighting of the pole facilitates its raising and lowering. On the pole is a 'tree' of five branches on each of which are placed several 'birds.' These birds are now usually made of plastic, but at various times in the past have been made of wood, wire or cork and feathers. At the very top of the 'tree' is placed a large 'bird,' known as the 'king bird.' The other 'birds' are placed on the branches.

Belgian pole archery

The object of the game is to shoot down these 'birds' with bow and arrow. The bow used is the traditional bow of wood or fibreglass, but the arrow has a flat head instead of a sharp point. The players stand beside the pole, which is tilted very slightly towards them, and take turns in shooting upwards to dislodge the 'birds.' The archers are sheltered from their falling arrows by a screen behind which they retreat after shooting. Points are assigned to each 'bird,' the 'king bird' being the most valuable. The winner is the archer who has accumulated most points when all the 'birds' have been shot down.

In Manitoba today, tournaments held each summer attract a great number of participants. The sport is, however, largely confined to people of Belgian origin, as most other archers prefer the English style of archery.

Another favourite outdoor sport is bicycling. The Belgians cannot claim credit for introducing this to Manitoba, for the French had organized it in the late 1870's. The Belgians, however, were mainly responsible for the sport's popularity. They formed the St. Boniface Cycling Club in 1916 and later, in the 1930's, built a dirt-track velodrome where races were held every Sunday. Prior to the Second World War bicycle races were regularly held on Wilkes Avenue in what is now Tuxedo, and long distance races were organized between Winnipeg and such places as Kenora and Winnipeg Beach. The record the the race to Winnipeg Beach was set in 1934 when Theodore Dubois covered the 46 miles in one hour and 40 minutes.

Of the various individual races, one of the most popular was the 'Miss and Out' or 'Devil take the hindmost' race.

In this the last rider across the tape at the end of each lap is eliminated until only two riders remain.

After the war the popularity of the sport declined, although in recent years interest has again increased. The Belgian Club now co-sponsors an annual race on Victoria Day in St. Boniface, but ironically the great majority of the participants are non-Belgians.

Cyclists leaving the city for Winnipeg Beach, 1932

The most popular Belgian indoor sport played in Manitoba is Belgian bowling. There are two versions, ladies' and men's, but neither has much in common with the more widespread five-pin and ten-pin bowling.

The ladies' version of the game is played on a flat alley about 20 feet long, at each end of which is a metal hoop. The players take turns rolling a conventional five-pin bowl down the alley in an attempt to get it through the hoop. When the players have each had a turn, they change ends and repeat the process. The very simplicity of this version of the game has militated against its popularity, so that today it is seldom played either in Manitoba or Belgium.

The men's version is still popular, however, even with the ladies. It combines elements of curling and horseshoes, and is known as bowling simply because it is played with a bowl. The bowl, made of a hard rubber substance and about seven inches in diameter, is bevelled and weighs almost ten pounds. It looks very like a flat cheese, about 4 inches thick. The game is played on a dirt alley about 35 feet long and 12 feet wide. Two wooden pegs about nine inches tall are placed 27 feet apart, about four feet from each end. The alley is slanted slightly to the middle to allow the bowls to curve more easily when rolled.

The rules of the game are fairly simple, and competition may take place in singles, doubles, or in teams of three, four or five, but it is usually played by teams of three. The object of the game is to roll the bowl as close as possible to the peg at the far end of the alley. At the start of the game the teams toss a coin to decide which team bowls first; subsequently, the winners of the previous end bowl

first. In singles competition, however, the two players alter-
nate.

In the team game, the first player stands by the peg
and bowls. The first player of the opposing team then
attempts, as in curling, either to roll his bowl closer to
the peg than his opponent or to knock his opponent's bowl
away with a fast shot. After each member of both teams
has bowled, the team which has rolled the bowl closest
to the peg scores one point. The teams then go to the
opposite end of the alley and repeat the process. This
continues until one team has earned 12 points and wins
the game. Three games constitute a match. In tournaments,
each team continues to play until it loses a match.

In Winnipeg the game is played indoors at the Belgian
Club which has two alleys. In some small towns it is played
outside during the summer, but indoor alleys have recently
been constructed at Holland and Swan Lake. The game
was introduced to Manitoba by the first Belgian immigrants
and was well developed by the 1920's. By the 1950's the
Manitoba League consisted of as many as 18 clubs from
across the province. The centre of bowling, however, is still
the Belgian Club which sponsors four provincial tournaments each year. While Manitobans of Belgian origin are
showing renewed interest in the sport, participants are now
increasingly drawn from other ethnic groups.

One game which was played more for enjoyment than
competition was Belgian darts. Although popular in the
past, this game is now seldom played probably because
of the difficulty of obtaining the necessary equipment.

The Belgian dartboard is quite different from its English
counterpart. Whereas the English version is a circle divided

into radian sections, the Belgian board consists of a series of five concentric coloured circles, much like a traditional rifle-range target, with a bull's-eye in the centre. Each circle has a points value. The bull's-eye is valued at 50; while the value of the circles ranges in sets of five from 25 for the inmost circle to five for the outside. The bull's-eye is about ¾ inches in diameter; while the entire board is only nine inches, considerably smaller than the English version.

The rules of the game are very simple. Play takes place in singles, each player having four darts. Standing six feet from the target, each player throws four darts and the points are added. This continues for ten rounds, at the end of which the player with the higher score wins the game.

The game of Belgian darts was brought to Manitoba by immigrants in the 1920's, and was more formally organized by the St. Boniface Dart Club which was established in 1935. The popularity of the game was at its height before the Second World War when many young Belgians played it in corner stores or anywhere that a dartboard could be set up. Regular tournaments were held for several years in St. Boniface, but the game never became popular in other Belgian communities in Manitoba. An annual tournament still takes place in St. Boniface and attracts about 50 participants, but between tournaments the game is rarely played.

Belgian immigrants to Manitoba also brought with them two rather complicated Flemish card games.

The first of these is called 'bieden' which in Flemish means 'to bid.' This is usually contracted to 'bien.' Somewhat similar to the game of bridge, it is played by two sets of partners with a deck of cards from which all cards from two to six inclusive have been removed. Each set of partners receives an initial 16 match points, and the object is to get rid of these by winning games. The dealer deals the cards, four at a time, to each player; and the player to the left of the dealer then opens the bidding. The player is guided in his bidding by the number of 'meld' or 'show' points he has in his hand and what he thinks are in his partner's hand. These points are calculated as follows: a run of three counts 20, a run of four 50, and a run of five 100. If the player has the king and queen included in a run, he may add 20 extra points. Four queens, four kings or four aces count as 100, and four jacks as 200. There is a standard system for bidding; if the player has 20 'show' points, he bids 60; if 50, he bids 90; and if 100, he bids 180. Bidding continues until all players agree that no one can bid any higher.

At this point, the player with the highest bid plays his first card, the suit to which this card belongs remaining the trump suit throughout the game. The points value of each card is calculated as follows: an ace is always worth 11, a king three, and a queen two. When in trump, a jack is worth 20, but when not in trump is worth only one point. A ten is always worth ten points; while a nine is 14 when in trump but otherwise worthless. Sevens and eights are always worthless.

The player to his left plays his best card, and so the game continues. If a player sees that he cannot possibly win the trick, he plays a scrap card (a seven or eight, or a nine when not in trump). After each player has played one card, the player with the best card wins the trick. This is repeated until all cards have been played. At this point, the player with the highest bid adds the number of points in the tricks he has won to those in his partner's. He then adds these to the number of 'show' points which he and his partner held originally. If the total equals or exceeds the number of points in the original bid, he and his partner win the game and lose some match points. If the total falls short of the original bid, they lose the game and gain some match points, while their opponents lose an equal number of match points.

The number of match points lost or gained is determined by the number of points the player has bid, with each set of 50 game points worth one match point. For example, if a player bids 200 and earns 210, he subtracts four match points from the 16 with which he started.

The match continues until one set of partners has disposed of its 16 match points. In addition to achieving this in the normal way, there are two methods of bringing quick victory. The first of these is the 'pandoer' in which the player gambles on winning all the tricks in the game. If successful, he and his partner get rid of half their match points; it not, they gain half and their opponents lose half. The second method is known as the 'zuiver pandoer,' 'bloten pandoer,' or 'pandoer op tafel,' and can be used if all the player's cards are trumps. The player simply states his intention and places his cards on the table. By doing so, the player gets rid of all his match points and therefore wins the match.

Although the game has virtually disappeared in Belgium, it has enjoyed an increasing popularity in Manitoba where it is played by members of all ethnic groups. Traditionally, the game is never played for money but for drinks, with the stakes determined solely by the players' thirst.

The second Flemish card game is a version of whist which, though still popular in Belgium, is now seldom played in Manitoba. This is probably because of the complexity of the game which is even more complicated than 'bien.' While similar to 'bien,' it differs in that a player may play with or without a partner, may change partners in the middle of the game, may trade cards, and may win a game either by winning tricks, or if he has low cards, by losing all the tricks in a game.

Another traditional recreation worthy of passing mention is the pipe-smoking competition. These contests were at first held monthly during the fall and winter both in the city and country towns. Using long clay pipes imported from Belgium and fine cut cigarette tobacco, each contestant attempted to keep his pipe continuously alight longer than the others. The record stands at 106 minutes. Each contestant originally paid a 10¢ entry fee, but when this was raised to 25¢ the competition became less popular. Today there is only one annual competition, and interest in that has virtually ended.

Apart from participating in specific sports and games, the Belgians also actively continue the centuries-old 'kermis' or festival. Kermis Week is now an annual event usually held at the Belgian Club during the third week of February. It is a traditional week of festivities which attracts Belgians from all parts of the province to share in sports and feasting. This, more than any other single event, has served to keep alive the traditional spirit of the Belgians in Manitoba.

CHAPTER VII

Past, Present and Future

LIKE all immigrants, the Belgians came for a variety of reasons. Some came for economic benefit, escaping the densely populated homeland with its limited future for the seemingly boundless land and opportunities offered by the young and growing province of Manitoba. Some were lured by the glowing reports of immigration agents or relations who had already achieved success here. Still others sought adventure and had been dissuaded by their families from emigration to the Congo.

These early immigrants differed in material wealth, in education and sometimes in language but they were united in their religious faith and they shared the characteristics of hard work, adaptability, independence and thrift.

As a group, they adapted readily to their new homeland and were generally well received by others. While to some extent the Walloons tended to merge with the French-speaking population, the Flemish Belgians mixed equally well with the English-speaking groups and later tended to adopt the English language.

With a gradual trend towards assimilation into the dominant English culture, the Belgians suffered little overt discrimination. Their reputation as hard workers, their

individuality, their practicality and their adaptability made
them ideal employees. Moreover, their comparatively small
numbers, their generally passive role in politics and their
lack of concern for ethnic identity posed no threat to provincial society.

Over the years, however, these very characteristics, which
initially made them so welcome as immigrants, have gradually eroded the Belgian sense of identity and have virtually
destroyed the Flemish language among the younger generation.

Today there is a serious split within the Belgian
community. It is not the historic ethnic and linguistic di-
chotomy between Fleming and Walloon, but rather a split
of generations. It is perfectly natural that the younger
generation yearns for a knowledge and understanding of
its cultural traditions. The tragedy lies in the decline of
the Flemish language, for language is the key to cultural
appreciation. Without knowledge of the Flemish language,
the younger Belgians are effectively cut off from their
cultural inheritance. The blame for this must surely be
shared by both old and young: the old for failing to pass
on their language, and the young for failing to show greater
initiative in seeking to learn it.

What of the future? While there are signs of a resurgence
of Belgian self-identity and pride, there is little evidence
of a strong linguistic revival. Without that, it is doubtful
if the traditional culture will survive this generation. But
how seriously do Belgians want a distinct identity? If they
do, a much more consistent and determined effort is an
urgent necessity, for without it the quickening trend
towards total assimilation will inevitably be completed, and

a small but significant part of the Manitoba cultural mosaic will have been lost. That would be a loss not only to the Belgians but to all who truly appreciate the value of cultural diversity in the life of our province.

Appendix I

PRIESTS OF SACRED HEART PARISH

Father Evereard Kwakman	1918-1928
Father Adelard Couture	1928
Father Willibrord of Mortsel	1928
Father Chrysostom of Kalmthout	1928-1934
Father Damas Van Dycke	1934-1941
Father Peter Constandt	1941-1947
Father Henri Van Olffen	1947-1950
Father Mark Nelissen	1950-1952
Father Otger Devent	1952-1954
Father Damas Van Dycke	1954-1956
Father Peter Constandt	1956-1958
Father Aurèle Prefontaine	1958-1963
Father Germain Declerck	1963-1967
Father Omer Deroo	1967-1971
Father Leo Baert	1971-

Appendix II

PRESIDENTS OF THE BELGIAN CLUB

Louis De Nobele	1905-1907
Pierre Bossuyt	1907-1912
August Van Horenbeeck	1912-1914
Pierre Bossuyt	1914
Emile Elias	1914-1915
Alidor Van Elslander	1915-1917
August Van Horenbeeck	1917
Anthony Hoornaert	1917
Louis De Nobele	1917
August Janssens	1917-1919
Anthony Hoornaert	1919-1921
Alidor Van Elslander	1921-1926
Nicolas Pirotton	1926-1935
Alfred De Cruyenaere	1935-1938
Theodore Bockstael	1938-1946
Wilbur Van Walleghem	1946-1972
André Janssens	1972-1976
Wilbur Van Walleghem	1976-

Select Bibliography

Carson, Patricia, *The Fair Face of Flanders*.
(Ghent: E. Story — Scientia, 1969.)

Le Club Belge Fiftieth Anniversary 1905-1955.
(St. Boniface: Le Club Belge, 1955.)

Le Club Belge: Minutes of the Executive Committee and General Meetings.

Les Belges au Manitoba. Lettres Authentiques de Colons Belges au Manitoba. (Ottawa: Imprimerie de l'Etat, 1894.)

Lyon, Margot, *Belgium*.
(London: Thames & Hudson, 1971.)

Mallinson, Vernon, *Belgium*.
(New York: Praeger, 1970.)

Roy, Marie-Anna A., *La Montagne Pembina au temps des colons* (n.p. 1970).

Théoret, Anatole E., *Sainte-Rose-du-Lac*.
(Sainte-Rose-du-Lac Parish, 1948.)

Wright, Norman E., *In View of the Turtle Hill*.
(Deloraine: Deloraine Times, 1951)

The Belgians in Manitoba

Keith Wilson
James B. Wyndels

Manitoba is justly proud of her ethnic and cultural groups. Of all the components of this mosaic, however, the Belgians are probably among the least known. This is partly because they form only a small percentage of the population, and partly because, for various reasons, they tend to lack identification as a distinct group.

This book, undertaken to mark the forthcoming 75th anniversary of The Belgian Club in St. Boniface, tells the story of the immigration of Belgians to Manitoba, and describes their activities, characteristics and contributions.

Intended for schools and for the general reader, the book is divided into seven chapters: Belgium: the historical background; Belgian immigration to Manitoba; Le Club Belge/ The Belgian Club; Religion, education and cultural activities; Occupations; Social life: sports and pastimes; Past, present and future